THE NEW
whole grains COOKBOOK

THE NEW

whole grains COOKBOOK

Terrific Recipes Using **Farro, Quinoa, Brown Rice, Barley,**
and **Many Other Delicious** *and* **Nutritious Grains**

by Robin Asbell

PHOTOGRAPHS *by* **CAREN ALPERT**

CHRONICLE BOOKS
SAN FRANCISCO

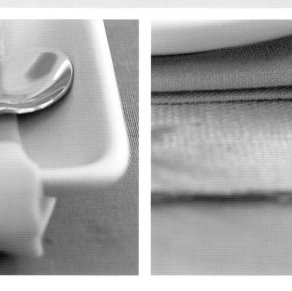

Library of Congress Cataloging-in-Publication
Data available.

ISBN 978-0-8118-5647-8

Manufactured in China.

Designed *by* **JAY PETER SALVAS**
Prop styling *by* **CAROL HACKER**
Food styling *by* **BASIL FRIEDMAN**
This book was typeset in **TRADE GOTHIC 9/12**
    and **FILOSOFIA 11/14**

Raw rice plants courtesy of **MASSA ORGANICS**,
Chico, California.

10 9 8 7 6 5 4 3 2

Chronicle Books LLC
680 Second Street
San Francisco, California 94107
WWW.CHRONICLEBOOKS.COM

ACKNOWLEDGMENTS

To Stan, the love of my life and my biggest fan, thanks for eating the same thing over and over until I got it right.

This book came into being because of Antonia Allegra and Nion McEvoy, and I thank both of them for believing in me. Working on the book with Amy Treadwell has been a wonderful experience.

My friends and family made the writing life possible, and their support keeps me going. Special thanks go to my client family, the people who tasted and praised these recipes more than anyone else. Your palates are a part of me, after all these years.

Table *of* Contents

BREAKFAST

BREADS FOR ALL TIMES OF DAY

WARM WHOLE SIDES

COLD WHOLE SIDES

WHOLE SOUPS AND DUMPLINGS

WHOLE ENTRÉES

Introducing Whole Grains

Everything old is new again. Ancient foods, once discarded on the road to progress, have come back into vogue. It turns out that the very old-fashioned habit of filling up on unrefined grains still suits the human body perfectly. Many of the grains I will be discussing in this book have been cultivated for thousands of years, and were the central nourishment for the cultures that flourished around the fields.

And yet many of you have never even heard of them. Rediscovering these delicious, beautiful foods is going to be fun.

In the last hundred years, our taste for refined foods has gotten the better of us. In stripping off the nutritious outer layers of the few grains we continue to consume, we throw out the minerals, antioxidants, and fiber, keeping only the quick-burning starches and a bit of protein. White bread and white rice are the only grains most Americans eat.

The evidence that we need to get back to the whole grain grows every day. In 2005, the U.S. Department of Agriculture changed its food pyramid and began urging Americans to eat at least three servings a day of whole grains, up from the paltry single serving it recommended previously. This change was in response to studies clearly indicating that consumption of whole grains lowers the risks of heart disease, cancer, diabetes, stroke, obesity, and other killers. We often hear about the fiber in grains, but that is only one of the important elements in the equation. Antioxidants, which work in the body to prevent cell damage, are also found in plant foods. Researchers at Cornell University found that whole grains are actually higher in antioxidants than fruits and vegetables are. Whole grains also contain the minerals that are deficient in the typical American diet. See "Whole-Grain Synergy" on page 12 for more science.

So why don't people eat enough whole grains? It all started during the Industrial Revolution. Whole grains, with their traces of good fats, spoil

more easily than refined ones. The bran layer on the outside of each grain and the germ at the tip, are where the essential fatty acids and enzymes are usually stored, along with the minerals and antioxidants. Milling the bran and germ away makes a starchy product that won't spoil. Once large-scale milling made white flour affordable, people could keep a bag of it on a shelf for years. "White" foods carried a cachet of refinement, even as they became cheap.

In the last few years, however, attitudes have changed. Now a grain like Purple Prairie barley or Job's tears commands a premium price and appears in tiny portions in the best restaurants. Chefs have discovered the subtle balance that can be created on the plate with these unique, flavorful foods. Unlike neutral starches, whole grains can even play a part in wine pairing, with earthy and sweet notes to complement the wine.

When it comes to whole grains, freshness matters. People who are used to shelf-stable white flours often forget that whole wheat and grains can actually spoil. Whole grains contain varying amounts of fat and enzymes that will go to work breaking down the grain at room temperature. Once the grains are ground to make flour, they are even more delicate, so unless you will be using them up within a month, keep them in the refrigerator or freezer.

On the physical level, sugar and white flour give us a rush. Contemporary science has brought us the glycemic index, a tool dietitians devised to help diabetics choose foods that would have the least impact on their blood sugar. The index rates foods on how much and how fast blood sugar rises when the food is eaten on an empty stomach. The high glycemic index rating of white flour and white rice means that they cause a spike in blood sugar, and then a rapid drop. Higher-fiber whole grains release carbohydrates more slowly into the gut. To simplify, stick to whole grains for slow-burning carbs.

If you are new to whole grains, you might want to make a gradual transition away from the soft, bland white ones. White flour is like a blank canvas, on which delicate washes of flavor, like butter and eggs, dominate. Without its hearty bran and germ, white flour is light and higher in gluten and is easy to leaven into airy constructs. Even so, balancing hearty flavors, adding a bit of gluten flour to breads, and just learning to love the sweet, nutty flavor of wheat are all easy to do. Wimpy white bread seems insubstantial once you are used to the real thing.

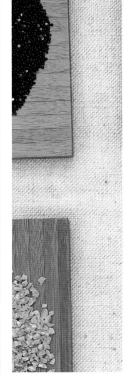

The place on your table currently occupied by white rice and pasta can easily be filled with hearty, delicious whole-grain dishes. Using the cooking charts on pages 24–25, start serving whole grains as a bed for your favorite stir-fries, curries, and saucy main dishes. Take care at first to make sure you cook them until they are fully tender, so your system will not be taxed by hard, undercooked grain. Once you've made this change, look to the recipes for creative ways to use whole grains in all sorts of dishes. Most of the recipes can be modified for vegetarians by using vegetable stocks and substituting tofu, tempeh, or mock meats.

The baking recipes in this book use only whole-grain flours. If you are new to this type of baking, you can easily substitute unbleached wheat flour for half of the whole wheat flour. The results will be lighter than the whole-grain version, but better for you than processed foods. As you fall in love with the flavor and heft of whole grains, gradually work up to all whole flours. The important thing is to get more whole grains and enjoy your food at the same time.

WHOLE-GRAIN SYNERGY

According to Leonard Marquart, PhD, RD, and professor at the University of Minnesota Department of Science and Nutrition, cancer rates would drop by up to 40 percent if whole grains replaced refined products. A very positive chain of events starts when these grains enter the digestive system. The fiber in grains contains proteins; starches; vitamins E and B complex, including folate; and minerals. Selenium and protective antioxidant chemicals are also carried by the fiber. As those are being absorbed, the carbohydrates, inulin, and fiber start to ferment, feeding the good bacteria in the gut. This activity lowers the pH of the colon and produces a compound called butyrate, both of which are associated with lowered cancer risk.

Fiber keeps the food moving more quickly through the colon, so that the unavoidable toxins in our food don't get absorbed into the body; it also dilutes them with its bulk. Our bodies naturally dump used hormones and bile acids in the gut to be excreted, and if fiber does not sweep them up and carry them away, they may be reabsorbed and increase the risk of cancer.

INTRODUCING WHOLE GRAINS

The Grains

WHOLE WHEAT COUSCOUS

Confusion reigns when it comes to couscous: Is it a chunk of grain or a pasta? Couscous is made from flour—in this case, whole semolina wheat flour—in an abbreviated version of pasta making. The flour is mixed with water, rubbed to form chunks, dried, and then sieved to sort it by size, so it will cook evenly. In the Mediterranean countries of its origin, couscous is traditionally made by hand, and dried couscous is rehydrated in a process of moistening, steaming, pouring out, moistening, and steaming again over a simmering stew, all in the pursuit of a light, fluffy result. The whole wheat couscous you will find in this country is medium-grain, and you can cook it simply by pouring a hot liquid and a dab of oil over it and letting it infuse for 5 minutes. You can also rehydrate it in stages at room temperature by sprinkling it with some of the required liquid, letting it absorb, fluffing, and repeating until you've added all the liquid.

BULGUR

Bulgur, also known as burghul or bulgar, is the result of an ancient food preservation technique practiced in the Near East and Mediterranean region. At harvest, fresh, unhusked wheat is boiled, then dried, husked, and cracked. This process drives nutrients from the bran deeper into the grain. Middle Eastern groceries sell varying sizes of bulgur, which are traditionally used in different dishes. Some of these imported bulgurs are slightly refined, with a pale appearance because they have had some bran removed, so stick with the darker, whole-looking ones. Most of the bulgur sold in natural foods stores is the large variety, which is used for pilafs and tabouli. Because of the precooking of the wheat, bulgur is quick to rehydrate.

QUINOA

This "pseudograin" from the Peruvian Andes is not really a grain; instead it is in the goosefoot family, whose members include lamb's-quarters, spinach, and chard. The ancient Incas called it the "mother grain." When the Spaniards took over, they banned it, and it reverted to growing wild. It was introduced to U.S. stores in the 1980s. Like its leafy cousins, quinoa is high in calcium, iron, and B vitamins. It also possesses an unusually large, nutrient-rich germ, visible as the white circles that cling to each grain and fall off when it is cooked. Its amino acid balance is higher in lysine than other grains, making it a relatively complete protein. Although quinoa is a high-protein grain, ranging from 7.5 to 22 percent protein versus the 14 percent protein of hard wheat, it is gluten-free. It is also one of the few grains that can be popped simply by heating it in a dry pan.

The quinoa plant naturally coats the seed with a bitter layer of saponins to deter foraging animals. Most of the quinoa you will find has been washed to remove this soapy, gray-looking coat. If your quinoa is unwashed, you will see a soapy residue on the surface of the water when you wash it.

AMARANTH

Amaranth is another goosefoot family "pseudograin," grown by the ancient Aztecs in Central America for at least five thousand years. Amaranth is also grown for its intensely nutritious leaves. Like quinoa, it is high in protein and good fats and is gluten-free. Cooking with amaranth is more of a challenge than cooking with quinoa, because the tiny, 1- to 2-millimeter seeds stay crunchy while producing a porridgey consistency all around them. The Aztecs popped the seeds and mixed them with sweet syrups, a treat still made in Mexico called *alegria*. The seeds can be steeped or added raw to baked goods for crunch.

TEFF

Teff originated in Ethiopia, and its name translates to "lost," because the tiny coffee-brown, red, or ivory seeds, half as big as amaranth, are hard to see. Teff is nearly wild and grows in tough, arid conditions. Maturing in 120 days, the high-calcium, mineral-rich crop was survival food for thousands of years. It was primarily ground into flour for *injera*, the traditional crêpelike flatbread used as both serving plate and edible spoon in Ethiopian dining. Today, because it is labor-intensive and expensive, teff has been replaced with refined flours, and most restaurants here cut the teff used in injera with millet or wheat. Teff has its own indigenous yeast on the grain, so mixing fresh teff flour with water and letting it ferment will produce a consistent sourdough batter for injera. With no bitter flavors, teff is quite tasty in stews and breads, and is gluten-free.

MILLET

This hardy grain has been cultivated in Asia and Africa for six thousand years. Able to survive with the least amount of water and soil nutrients of any grain, millet is 16 to 22 percent protein. It can be popped and, if pretoasted, will cook up into a fluffy golden pilaf. Millet is one of the most delicate grains, and it can be manipulated by cooking to make very different textures. Untoasted millet can be very soft and is perfect for purées, molded croquettes, and polenta-style preparations, as well as eating with the fingers. After some years on the list of forbidden foods for the gluten-intolerant, millet was declared gluten-free in 2000 by the U.S. government.

BUCKWHEAT

Despite the word "wheat" in the name, buckwheat is not related to wheat or any grain. It's another pseudograin and is genetically close to rhubarb and sorrel. Gluten-free buckwheat is native to Asia and matures in only two months, making it a popular crop in cold climates. Its high B-vitamin, mineral, and vitamin E content makes it a great grain for vegetarians. The hulled buckwheat kernel is called a groat and is often sold pretoasted as kasha.

Toasting firms the delicate grain, which starts absorbing water immediately, so rinse and drain it as quickly as you can before adding it to hot liquids.

BARLEY

Barley was one of the most revered crops in Stone Age China, and it returns to stardom today with the lowest glycemic index rating of any grain. Unrefined hulled barley is hard to find, but it is worth the effort for its slow-burning energy. Most barley is "pearled," a process that grinds off 33 percent of the grain. Barley does contain gluten.

Recently, an ancient barley known as Purple Prairie barley has come on the market, with a purple-pigmented bran layer. Black barley is also pigmented and higher in antioxidants than regular barley.

JOB'S TEARS

Job's tears, or *hato mugi*, is sometimes called Chinese barley, because its shape is similar to that of barley when pearled, but it is from a different family than barley. Job's tears is imported from Japan and China, so it is a bit pricey, but it is worth every penny. It can be found in the macrobiotic section of your natural foods store. The fat grains cook up to a texture remarkably similar to that of chestnuts. *Yuuki*, the least pearled hato mugi, has the most brown bran layer intact. Job's tears is recommended for clearing the skin, easing joint pain, and promoting weight loss in traditional Chinese medicine.

RICES

The world of rice is a sprawling and colorful one, with a hundred thousand varieties of rice grown globally and a history of cultivation stretching back to 7000 B.C. Whole-grain brown, red, purple, and black rices are what we will be cooking in this book. Each variety of rice is unique and will cook to a slightly different texture than the others, so you will have quite an adventure trying them all.

Brown rice is either long-, medium-, or short-grain. Long-grain rices are higher in amylose, the more absorbent, firmer starch in all rice, while medium- and short-grain rices are higher in amylopectin, the stickier starch. Amylose starch cooks at a higher temperature than amylopectin, and cultures that prefer these rices use different cooking techniques. Sticky or sweet rice is available in brown and black varieties and is the highest in amylopectin. Because of the bran holding the starch in, these qualities are less pronounced in whole-grain rices than in their naked counterparts. "Aromatic" varieties like basmati and jasmine are available brown. Kalijira is known as "baby basmati," and the short, narrow grains, resembling miniature basmati, cook in 25 minutes. Jasmine is a

rare exception to the rule, with long grains that are higher in amylopectin, making jasmine a soft rice.

Pigmented rices are black, purple, red, and mahogany. Their color is caused by anthocyanin pigments in the outer bran, so they are the richest in antioxidants of any rices. These rices can range from long grain to short or sticky. Their place in history varies from the "forbidden" rice of China, which was reserved for the emperor, to the red rices of India, which were, until recently, resented for infiltrating basmati crops and sullying the whiteness of the product. I often pick up great bargains on pigmented rices at Asian markets, where they are labeled in languages I can't read. It's easy enough to figure out how to cook them. When you buy a rice, look at the shape of the grain. If it is short and stubby, use it in recipes where a little stickiness is nice. If it is long, add a little more water and use it in dishes where separate and fluffy is the name of the game. Rice blends often mix a few pigmented rices in with brown rice, for a variety of textures and to stretch the more expensive kinds.

WILD RICE

Mahnomen, as the Ojibway called wild rice, is not related to true rice but is an aquatic grass that originated in North American marshes. There are two very different types: the long, shiny black cultivated version and the mottled gray, hand-harvested original. The dark pigments are antioxidants as well as chlorophyll derivatives. The softer, hand-harvested gray wild rice will cook in 20 to 30 minutes, while the shiny, black cultivated kind can simmer for up to 2 hours before the grains start splitting. The only way to know with each batch of rice is to start checking and testing at 20 minutes.

WHEATS

The wheat berries you can buy whole are either soft wheat or hard red winter wheat. Soft wheat is lower in gluten and is used to make pastry flour, while hard wheat is higher in gluten and is used for bread flour. Kamut is an ancient relative of durum wheat and has large, golden grains and lots of gluten. Spelt is also a hard, high-protein wheat. Kamut and spelt are often used in baking as alternatives for people who are allergic to standard wheat, but people with gluten sensitivities can't tolerate them. Farro, an ancient Italian strain of wheat, is used in soups and risottos. A newly developed variety is white wheat, for whole-grain breads with no brown color.

OATS

Oats store their relatively high fat content and fat-digesting enzymes in the starchy endosperm instead of the germ, and that makes them vulnerable to rancidity. To combat this process, they are usually heat-treated and rolled, which also makes them cook more quickly. The fiber in the bran, called beta-glucans, cleans cholesterol from the body. Both oats and wheat are as high in antioxidant chemicals as broccoli and spinach. Whole oat grains cook up like wheat berries, and Scotch or steel-cut oats are just broken oats, chopped to allow the starches to spill out and to speed cooking.

The familiar rolled oats come in quick and old-fashioned styles. Quick oats have been processed in a way that changes the starches, giving them a higher glycemic index. The thicker and more lightly processed the oats are, the better they are for you, so look for old-fashioned, thick rolled oats, and try soaking them overnight to make a quick morning cereal.

RYE

Whole rye is another hardy grain that can grow in poor soils. It has a storied history in northern Europe, where rye became a staple after it was brought from Asia in 1000 B.C. Rye bread has the distinction of having been declared a "free food" by Weight Watchers in Finland, putting it in the same category as raw vegetables for unlimited snacking. It contains a special kind of carbohydrate called arabinoxylans, which absorb eight times its weight in water and hold it. This makes it a great hunger-filler, as well as keeping rye breads fresh longer. The rye starches also don't harden when cooled, as rice and other grains do. This softness makes it a great grain for chilled salads, as well as any wheat berry recipe.

GRAIN NUTRITION INFORMATION

AMARANTH (¼ *cup, 47 grams*) 180 calories, 3 grams fat, 31 grams carbohydrate, 7 grams protein, 170 milligrams potassium, iron 20%, calcium 8%, vitamin C 4%, riboflavin 6%, folate 6%

BARLEY, HULLED (¼ *cup, 46 grams*) 140 calories, 1 gram fat, 35 grams carbohydrate, 5 grams protein, iron 8%

BARLEY, PURPLE PRAIRIE (¼ *cup, 28 grams*) 101 calories, 1 gram fat, 20 grams carbohydrate, 4 grams protein, calcium 1.5%, iron 3.9%

BULGUR (¼ *cup, 44 grams*) 160 calories, 0.5 gram fat, 32 grams carbohydrate, 5 grams protein, 105 mg potassium, calcium 2%, iron 6%

COUSCOUS, WHOLE WHEAT (¼ *cup, 55 grams*) 210 calories, 1 gram fat, 45 grams carbohydrate, 8 grams protein, iron 10%

OATS, OLD-FASHIONED ROLLED (½ *cup, 40 grams*) 150 calories, 3 grams fat, 27 grams carbohydrate, 5 grams protein, calcium 2%, iron 10%

QUINOA (¼ *cup, 42 grams*) 166 calories, 3 grams fat, 30 grams carbohydrate, 5 grams protein, phosphorus 15%, iron 10%, riboflavin 8%

QUINOA, RED (¼ *cup, 42 grams*) 163 calories, 3 grams fat, 29 grams carbohydrate, 6 grams protein, calcium 2%, phosphorus 25%, iron 13%, riboflavin 10%

RICE BHUTANESE RED (¼ *cup, 45 grams*) 150 calories, 0 grams fat, 36 grams carbohydrate, 3 grams protein, iron 2%

RICE, BROWN BASMATI (¼ *cup, 46 grams*) 160 calories, 1.5 grams fat, 34 grams carbohydrate, 4 grams protein, iron 2%

RICE, BROWN SWEET (¼ *cup, 51 grams*) 180 calories, 1.5 grams fat, 40 grams carbohydrate, 4 grams protein, iron 4%

RICE, CHINESE BLACK (¼ *cup, 48 grams*) 160 calories, 1.5 grams fat, 34 grams carbohydrate, 5 grams protein, iron 4%

RICE, RED CARGO (¼ *cup, 50 grams*) 176 calories, 1.7 grams fat, 36.3 grams carbohydrate, 3.9 grams protein, phosphorus 10%

RICE, THAI BLACK SWEET (¼ *cup, 50 grams*) 173 calories, 1.5 grams fat, 35 grams carbohydrate, 4 grams protein, iron 5.5%, phosphorus 5.5%

RYE, WHOLE (¼ *cup, 47 grams*) 160 calories, 1 gram fat, 34 grams carbohydrate, 6 grams protein, calcium 2%, iron 10%

TEFF (¼ *cup, 45 grams*) 160 calories, 1 gram fat, 32 grams carbohydrate, 5 grams protein, iron 20%, thiamine 10%, calcium 8%

WEHANI (¼ *cup, 49 grams*) 170 calories, 1.5 grams fat, 38 grams carbohydrate, 3 grams protein, iron 4%

Cooking Grains

Grains can be cooked in many different ways, each with slightly different results. Each crop of grain will have slight variations, so there are no absolutes in cooking times and water measurements. Sturdy, whole "berries," like wheat and rye, and rices high in amylose will cook up separate and firm, but will soften a bit if simmered with more liquid for longer cooking times. More delicate grains, like buckwheat and millet, can be pretoasted or sautéed and then cooked in a little less water to keep them separate. They can also be simmered in more liquid to a porridge consistency, and even allowed to solidify for a polenta-style presentation. Tiny amaranth and teff will cook only to a porridge consistency, studded with tiny crunches, unless you pop them.

When preparing the recipes in the Cold Whole Sides chapter, serving freshly cooked grain, cooled to room temperature, is optimum. When grains other than rye are chilled, the starches harden in a process called retrogradation, and their tastes are muted. If you want to chill the salads, just let them sit out for a while before serving. If the grains are dressed and chilled overnight, they will absorb the dressing and need only a dash of oil to moisten them.

STEP ONE: CLEANING

Like any agricultural product, grains need to be cleaned. When using whole rice or a grain that you are not going to toast, simply put the grain in a large bowl and run cold water over it to a depth of about 3 inches above the surface of the grain. Massage it with your hand, keeping it to a quick swirl for buckwheat but scrubbing and massaging harder grains. Some chaff and broken kernels will float to the surface, so pour most of the water off and the floaters should go too. Then drain the grain in a wire-mesh strainer.

SOMETIMES: SOAKING

For many years, people were told to soak grains before cooking, in order to leach out the phytates, which were known to bind up the iron in grains and keep it from being absorbed by the body. Current research shows that phytates are valuable antioxidants, and that the iron binding is not really a problem, and so there is no nutritional reason to soak grains if you don't have time. Larger, long-cooking grains will benefit from an overnight soak, while just half an hour can make a positive difference in the tenderness of brown rice.

Soaked grains require less cooking time and liquid, and they turn out softer. This is not usually desired when cooking buckwheat, millet, or smaller grains, but seriously chewy grains seem to take forever to cook and never get quite as tender if they are not soaked. Grain that has soaked overnight will require about ¼ cup to ½ cup less cooking liquid per cup of grain, and about 10 minutes less cooking time. Sweet and short-grain rices are customarily soaked and then steamed.

SOMETIMES: TOASTING

Small, soft grains, notably millet and buckwheat, will stay more separate in cooking if their outer bran is hardened by the application of heat. They also develop a nutty flavor. Many chefs toast grains in a dry pan until they are crackling hot, to develop flavor. You can also spread them on a baking sheet and roast them. Some people try to wash grains and then pan-roast them, which is a good way to stick grains to the bottom of the pan and tear them to mush. I prefer to toast first, then quickly wash, and get them in the pan with hot liquids to cook.

Absorption

The cooking method that is most familiar to many of you is probably absorption. Measured liquid is put in the pot, with the grain either added then or when the liquid comes to a boil. Then the pot simmers, covered, until the liquid is absorbed. Adding the grain to cold liquid and bringing it up to temperature results in a softer grain, while adding it to boiling liquid makes the final result a bit firmer. Depending on your taste and the desired results, you can vary the amount of liquid. Each batch of grain can also be slightly different, so if you finish cooking a grain and it is too firm, just add some hot water and put it back on low.

Cooking liquids can be a big source of flavor, whether you use stock, fruit juices, or seasonings in the water. Experiment with adding spices and other flavorings to your cooking liquid, to complement the meal. With long-cooking grains, chopped vegetables and even whole cloves of garlic will cook to tenderness.

Baking

For large amounts of grain, baking is the best way to use the absorption method. It is easier to get even heat all around a big casserole in the oven than it is in a big pot on the stove. It's also a way to gently cook any amount of grain, and is handy when you are using all of your burners for other things.

Steaming

Steaming is the method used in Asian countries to cook glutinous rices or ones higher in amylopectin. Because these rices have starches that gelatinize at lower temperatures, they cook more evenly when soaked and steamed, a lower-temperature process. The rice is soaked overnight, drained, and then spread on a leaf, cheesecloth-lined grid, or basket and placed over simmering water. Whole-grain rices that respond to this treatment are glutinous black sticky rice, brown sweet rice, and short-grain brown rice. The gentle steam leaves them tender and not gummy. For more than a cup of rice, soak the rice overnight, and then spread cheesecloth on top of a bamboo steamer insert, put the drained rice on it in an even layer, and form a hole in the center for steam to pass through. Wrap the cheesecloth across the top of the rice, and steam until it is tender. Another method that works well with a smaller amount of rice is to put soaked rice in a heat-safe bowl, pour boiling water to the top of the grain, and steam over simmering water for 30 to 40 minutes.

Pasta-Style Coooking

Pasta-style cooking, which involves boiling grain in large amounts of water, is a fine way to cook really sturdy whole wheat and rye, or even wild rice, but it is not advisable for delicate buckwheat, and teff and amaranth are too tiny. I prefer the other methods when possible, as they allow the nutrients and pigments to be absorbed by the grains, rather than poured down the drain with the cooking water. Pasta-style cooking works for most grains, especially if you are unsure of the cooking time and are willing to test for doneness toward the end. When the grain is done, drain it, then put it back in the pan and let it stand off the heat, covered, for 10 minutes, for the final steam. The result will be a bit firmer than with absorption.

Pressure Cooking

Europeans have completely embraced the pressure cooker, and there is one in every kitchen. Despite great strides in pressure cooker design that make them very user-friendly, they have caught on with very few Americans.

That's a shame, because they shave time off the cooking of the big whole grains, and they cook very thoroughly. A flame tamer, or heat diffuser disk, is very helpful to prevent scorching when using a pressure cooker. As long as you have the right amount of water, the grains can be cooked to varying degrees of softness by manipulating the cooking time. Always use the "natural release" rather than the "quick release" method, to allow the grain to finish steaming as the pot depressurizes. Amaranth and teff are often not recommended for the pressure cooker because they might clog the valve, but in my own testing in a modern Kuhn Rikon 7-liter model, I had no problem with them.

AUTOMATIC RICE COOKERS

I love my rice cooker. I have a high-end "fuzzy logic" one with a brown rice setting, which takes about 2 hours, start to finish. It doesn't really save time, but it is completely hands-off, and it goes into keep-warm mode when it has finished. I also have a cheap "cook/keep warm" model, which can be used to cook whole grains as long as I make some adjustments and stay close so that I can turn it back on a few times. I have found that it does a nice job with millet and buckwheat on the white rice setting. It is key to know that the "cup" in the rice cooker or marked on the inside of the bowl is really a ¾-cup measurement. Use more water for brown rice in the cooker, and soak brown rice for at least half an hour before using a "cook/keep warm" model. Letting it stand in "keep warm" mode will finish the steaming.

ALWAYS: THE FINAL STEAM

In the absorption method, after all the water is absorbed into the grain, little holes form on the surface of the grains. Chinese cooks call them the "eyes" of the grain. Tip the pot slightly to see if any liquid is still loose in there, and if none rises up the side of the pot, take the pot off the heat and let it stand for 10 minutes. That final steam makes all the difference.

Equipment

For cooking grains, a few good tools will make your life easier. Most of the recipes call for a 1- or 2-quart heavy-bottomed saucepan with a tight-fitting lid. The heavy bottom is really important, and a good pan like All-Clad will keep grains from scorching as they absorb liquids. If you must use lighter pans, you can place an inexpensive device called a flame tamer or heat diffuser between the burner and the pan. These have saved many a pot of rice from sticking to the bottom. A wire-mesh strainer is absolutely necessary, so that you can wash your grains without pouring them down the drain. Beyond these essentials, pressure cookers and electric rice cookers are good investments, if you think you will use them. A good cast-iron Dutch oven, with a tight lid is also very useful. I recommend a Le Creuset Cocotte pan or, for a less expensive solution, a pre-seasoned Lodge Dutch oven.

GRAINS COOKING CHART

GRAIN	Precooking Techniques	Ratio of Liquid to Grain in a conventional pot (in a pressure cooker)	Cooking Time in a conventional pot for unsoaked grain (in a pressure cooker)
AMARANTH	None	2½ – 3 to 1 (2½ to 1)	25 minutes (15 minutes)
BLACK AND RED RICE	Can soak (see package for measurements)	generally 2 to 1	
BROWN KALIJIRA RICE	Can sauté	1¾ – 2 to 1 (1 cup plus 10 tablespoons to 1)	25 minutes (17 minutes)
BUCKWHEAT	Toast, sauté	1½ – 2 to 1 (2 to 1)	15 minutes (12 minutes)

GRAIN	Precooking Techniques	Ratio of Liquid to Grain in a conventional pot (in a pressure cooker)	Cooking Time in a conventional pot for unsoaked grain (in a pressure cooker)
BULGUR	Can sauté	1½ to 1 (not recommended)	10 minutes steaming (not recommended)
HULLED BARLEY, PURPLE or BLACK	Soaking recommended	2½ to 1 (1½ to 1)	1 hour (50 minutes)
LONG-GRAIN BROWN RICE	Can soak	1½ to 1 (1½ to 1)	40 to 45 minutes (35 minutes)
MILLET	Toast, sauté	1½ – 2½ to 1 (2 to 1)	20 minutes (12 minutes)
QUINOA	Can toast, sauté	1½ – 2 to 1 (1½ to 1)	15 minutes (10 minutes)
SHORT-GRAIN BROWN RICE	Can soak	2 to 1 (1½ to 1)	45 minutes to 50 minutes (35 minutes)
TEFF	None	3 to 1 (3 to 1)	20 minutes (8 minutes)
WHOLE OATS	Soaking recommended	2– 3 to 1 (1½–3 to 1)	1 hour (20 minutes)
WHOLE STICKY or SWEET RICE	Soaking recommended	2½ to 1 (2 to 1)	1 hour (40 minutes)
WHOLE WHEAT COUSCOUS	Can sauté	1½ to 1 (not recommended)	5 minutes steaming (not recommended)
WHOLE WHEAT FARRO, KAMUT, RYE	Soaking recommended	2 to 1 (1½ to 1)	1 hour (40 minutes)

BREAKFAST

MAKE THIS UNCOOKED MUESLI AT THE BEGINNING OF THE WEEK, and have it for breakfast for a few days. Thick rolled oats have a wonderful texture, and their starches are less gelatinized than quick oats, giving them a lower glycemic index.

½   cup **slivered almonds**

2   medium **apples**

1½ cups **nut milk** *or* other milk

2   tablespoons **maple syrup**

1½ cups **thick rolled oats**

¼   cup **soy protein powder**
     (*optional*)

½   cup **pitted dates**

OVERNIGHT APPLE-DATE MUESLI
WITH **NUT MILK**

Preheat the oven to 325°F, and spread the almonds on a baking pan. Bake for 10 minutes, just until golden. Let cool.

Get out a large storage tub or a bowl and quarter the apples, removing the cores but leaving the skin. Grate the apples into the bowl, and then add all of the remaining ingredients, including the almonds. Cover tightly and put in the refrigerator overnight, or for at least 8 hours.

Stir and serve cold, or microwave for 2 minutes per bowl.

SWEET BREAKFAST TABOULI WITH DRIED PLUMS

TABOULI SALAD IS A FAVORITE IN SUMMERTIME, so why not have a sweet version for breakfast? Hearty whole-grain bulgur is parboiled, driving all the nutrients into the nutty-tasting grains. Cooking it in apple juice gives it a tangy sweetness, as well as more nutrients.

½ cup **dried plums** *or* other dried fruit

2 tablespoon **dried mint flakes**, *or* ½ cup fresh mint

1 cup **apple juice**

½ cup **bulgur** *or* **whole wheat couscous**

2 tablespoons **fresh lemon juice**

2 tablespoons **honey**

1 teaspoon **flax oil** *or* rice bran oil

Chop the dried plums *(or other fruit and the fresh mint, if using).* In a storage tub or small casserole with a tight-fitting lid, mix the chopped plums and dried mint.

In a small saucepan, bring the apple juice to a boil and add the bulgur. Return to a boil, then reduce to a simmer and cover tightly. Simmer for 10 minutes, until the juice is absorbed and the bulgur is tender. *(If using couscous, pour the couscous into the boiling juice, stir, and take off the heat.)* Let stand to steam for 10 minutes. Scrape the bulgur into the tub with the plums and mint. Stir, and cover to steam the fruit. Chill for later use, or serve warm.

To serve, in a small cup, stir together the lemon juice, honey, and oil. Drizzle over the bulgur and fluff to mix.

CHUNKY APPLE-ALMOND GRANOLA
WITH **VARIATIONS**

IF YOU WANT TO AVOID REFINED SUGAR, try this fruit-sweetened granola. Rolled oats drink up the apple juice and become tender, then bake to crispness. Oats for breakfast are a popular way to lower cholesterol, but this granola is a great snack or dessert, too.

5 cups **old-fashioned rolled oats**	¼ teaspoon **salt** *(optional)*
1 cup **nonfat powdered milk**	1½ cups **apple juice concentrate** *(1 can)*, thawed
1 tablespoon **ground cinnamon**	2 teaspoons **vanilla extract**
2 cups **whole almonds**, very coarsely chopped	¼ cup **vegetable oil**

Preheat oven to 300°F. Spray or rub a rimmed sheet pan with vegetable oil spray. In a large bowl, mix the oats, milk powder, cinnamon, almonds, and salt, if using. In a small bowl, mix the juice concentrate, vanilla, and oil. Mix the liquid into the oat mixture, stirring with your hands.

Spread the oat mixture on the sprayed pan and bake for 30 minutes, then use a metal spatula to turn over portions of the mixture in the pan. Bake for another 30 minutes, and repeat. Bake for another 20 to 30 minutes. Let cool on a rack until completely cool and dry. Transfer to an airtight storage container or zipper-top bag.

Serve 1 cup granola with ¼ cup of the dried fruit of your choice, with skim milk or nonfat yogurt.

IF YOU ARE HAVING A SPECIAL BREAKFAST OR BRUNCH, here is a special granola to serve. It's also great layered in yogurt or ice cream parfaits, or just eaten by the handful. Use hearty old-fashioned rolled oats; they will be barely toasted and coated with caramelized sugar.

CARAMEL WALNUT CHOCOLATE CHUNK GRANOLA

4	cups **old-fashioned rolled oats**
1	cup **walnuts**, broken into large pieces
¼	teaspoon **salt**
¼	cup **water**
1	cup **sugar**
¼	cup **butter**, sliced
1	teaspoon **vanilla extract**
1	cup **dark chocolate chunks** (*about 4 ounces*)

Line 2 large, rimmed baking sheets with parchment paper, and spray the parchment with vegetable oil spray. Preheat the oven to 300°F. In a large bowl, mix the oats, nuts, and salt. In a 2-quart heavy-bottomed saucepan, stir together the water and sugar. Over high heat, bring to a boil, moving the pan to keep it mixed, rather than stirring. Cook until the syrup turns a medium amber, then take it off the heat and add the butter carefully—it will foam and bubble. Stir in the butter with a heat-safe spatula, and then stir in the vanilla. Scrape into the oat mixture and stir immediately. The caramel mixture will start to harden and clump, but it will melt while baking and disperse.

Scrape the oat mixture onto the prepared pans, and spread it out into rough chunks. Bake for 15 minutes, then stir well. The caramel will be liquefied and soaking into the oats more evenly. Bake for 15 minutes more.

Remove to cooling racks. When cool, break the granola into chunks, mix with the chocolate chunks, and store in jars or zipper-top bags.

HAVE YOU NOTICED HOW TINY THE STORE-BOUGHT GRANOLA BARS HAVE GOTTEN? Just like fresh-baked cookies or breads, your homemade granola bars will blow away the packaged ones. Make a batch for breakfast, although you may find that they disappear at all hours of the day.

MAPLE-CINNAMON GRANOLA BARS

1 cup **old-fashioned rolled oats**	½ teaspoon **ground cinnamon**
½ cup **crisped brown rice cereal**	¼ teaspoon **salt**
¼ cup **whole wheat flour**	¼ cup **peanut butter**
¼ cup **brown sugar**	½ cup **maple syrup**
¼ cup **soy protein powder** *or* nonfat powdered milk	1 teaspoon **vanilla extract**
	2 tablespoons **canola oil**

Preheat the oven to 350°F. Lightly oil an 8-inch square baking pan. In a large bowl, mix the oats, rice cereal, flour, brown sugar, soy powder, cinnamon, and salt. In a small bowl or food processor, whisk together or process the peanut butter, maple syrup, vanilla, and canola oil until smooth. Stir the wet mixture into the dry one, and use your hands to combine them thoroughly.

Scrape the mixture into the prepared pan, and use wet hands to pat it evenly into the pan. Bake for 20 minutes. Using a bench knife or stiff metal spatula, cut into 8 bars by dividing it into 4 one way, then cutting it in half in the other direction. Put the pan back in the oven for 5 minutes. The bars should be golden brown. Let cool completely, then carefully cut the bars apart and separate them from the edges of the pan before removing. Store in a tightly closed tub or bag for up to a week, or freeze for a month.

OVERNIGHT SMOKED SALMON–SPINACH STRATA
WITH **WHOLE WHEAT**

USE UP LEFTOVER BREAD IN THIS TASTY BREAKFAST STRATA. This is a flexible recipe, so whatever pan size you have, just make a single layer of bread and whisk up enough egg mixture to cover everything. Make sure you use lox, not hot-smoked salmon chunks, which will become too tough during baking.

4 cups **cubed whole wheat bread** (*6 to 8 ounces*)	2 ounces **Gruyère cheese,** shredded
½ teaspoon **celery seeds**	6 large **eggs**
10 ounces **frozen spinach**, thawed *and* wrung out to remove excess liquid	1 cup **skim milk**
½ cup **slivered scallions**	¼ teaspoon **ground nutmeg**
4 ounces **thinly sliced lox,** chopped	¼ teaspoon **freshly cracked black pepper**
	¼ teaspoon **salt**
	Hot sauce to taste

Spray a 9-inch square or 8-by-12-inch casserole dish with vegetable oil spray, and lay the bread in the bottom. Scatter the celery seeds and spinach over it, then top with the scallions, lox, and cheese.

In a large bowl, whisk the eggs, then whisk in the milk, nutmeg, pepper, salt, and a few dashes of hot sauce. Pour over the casserole. Cover and chill for at least 8 hours or up to 24 hours.

Preheat the oven to 350°F. Bake the strata, uncovered, for 55 minutes, or until a knife inserted near the center comes out clean. Press down on the center of the strata with a spoon, and if any wet eggs rise into the depression, bake it a little longer. Let stand for 5 to 10 minutes before slicing.

THESE TENDER SCONES ARE LIGHTLY SWEETENED WITH MAPLE SYRUP and topped with crunchy streusel. The whole-grain and nut combination is classic, but you can substitute dried fruits for the nuts as well.

WHOLE WHEAT WALNUT SCONES WITH **STREUSEL**

STREUSEL

3 tablespoons **whole wheat pastry flour**

2 tablespoons **butter**, melted

5 tablespoons **maple sugar chunks**

1 teaspoon **ground cinnamon**

½ cup **finely chopped walnuts**

For the streusel topping, mix the flour, melted butter, maple sugar, cinnamon, and walnuts in a medium bowl and reserve.

For the scones, preheat the oven to 425°F. Line a baking sheet with parchment or spray with vegetable oil spray. In a large bowl, whisk the flour, baking powder, and salt. Grate or cut the butter with a pastry cutter, chopping the butter into small bits. In a small bowl, whisk the eggs and add ½ cup of the cream (reserving the rest), the maple syrup, and the vanilla. Mix well.

SCONES

3 ¼ cups **whole wheat pastry flour**

1 tablespoon **baking powder**

½ teaspoon **salt**

½ cup **cold butter**

2 large **eggs**

½ cup plus **2** tablespoons **heavy cream** *or* buttermilk, divided

½ cup **maple syrup**

½ teaspoon **vanilla extract**

1 cup **walnuts**, coarsely chopped

Make a well in the dry mixture and pour in the wet mixture. Stir just until mixed, then stir in the walnuts. Divide the dough in half. Dump it out onto a floured counter and shape each half into a circle ¾ inch thick. Slice each round, like a pie, into 6 wedges. Place each scone onto the prepared baking sheet with at least 1 inch between them. Brush the tops of the scones with the remaining 2 tablespoons cream, and press the streusel mixture on top. Bake for 15 to 18 minutes, until golden. Transfer to a wire rack to cool.

SAUCE

2	cups	**blueberries,** fresh *or* frozen
¼	cup	**sugar**
1	tablespoon	**lemon juice**

PANCAKES

1	cup	**whole wheat pastry flour**
½	cup	**wheat germ**
¼	cup	**sugar**
1	teaspoon	**baking powder**
½	teaspoon	**baking soda**
¼	teaspoon	**salt**
1¼	cups	**buttermilk**
¼	cup	**canola oil**
2	large	**eggs,** separated
2	cups	**sliced banana, berries,** *or* **raisins**
2	cups	**low-fat vanilla yogurt**

BUTTERMILK WHEAT GERM PANCAKES
WITH **YOGURT** AND **BLUEBERRY SAUCE**

THE NUTTY, SWEET PRESENCE OF WHEAT GERM MAKES THESE PANCAKES SPECIAL. Wheat germ is rich in the essential fats that make wheat so healthful, so buy it raw and keep it in the refrigerator or freezer.

For the sauce, in a medium saucepan mix the berries, sugar, and lemon juice. Heat over medium heat, stirring constantly, until it comes to a boil. Remove from the heat. The sauce will thicken as it stands.

For the pancakes, preheat the oven to 200°F. Mix the flour, wheat germ, sugar, baking powder, baking soda, and salt in a large bowl. Mix the buttermilk, oil, and egg yolks in a large measuring cup. Beat the egg whites to stiff peaks, using an electric mixer. Mix the yolk mixture into the dry ingredients just until moistened, then fold in the whites.

Heat a nonstick skillet or griddle over medium heat until hot. Lightly grease the skillet with spray vegetable oil or butter, and then drop ⅓-cup portions of batter on the skillet, spreading them a bit if thick. Drop fruit onto the pancakes, and press it down. Reduce the heat to medium-low. Cook until bubbly, turn, and cook for a couple minutes more. Transfer to an oven-safe platter and hold in the oven until all of the pancakes are done.

Serve the pancakes topped with yogurt and the blueberry sauce.

CHAPTER

2

BREADS FOR ALL TIMES OF DAY

THESE THIN BREADS ARE SOMEWHERE BETWEEN CRÊPES AND CHAPATIS. With no kneading or rolling, the batter is easy to whisk together, and the breads cook quickly on the stovetop. Feel free to flavor them as you see fit, with spices and herbs to go with the meal, or with different whole-grain flours. For a gluten-free bread, just use brown rice or bean flour instead of wheat. Try them with the Spicy Yellow Split Pea Quinoa Dal (*page 102*) and some chutney.

QUICK SKILLET FLATBREADS

½ cup **whole wheat pastry flour**

1 cup **oat, millet, teff,**
   or **amaranth flour**

¼ to ½ teaspoon **salt**, to taste

¼ teaspoon **baking soda**

1 cup **plain yogurt**, any type

1 cup plus **2** tablespoons **water**,
   plus more if needed

In a large bowl, combine the flours, salt, and baking soda. In a cup, whisk the yogurt and water together, then stir into the dry mixture. Add additional water, if needed, to make a batter with the consistency of heavy cream. Cover and let stand for half an hour.

Heat a nonstick, 10-inch sauté pan over high heat, and use a paper towel to smear just a bit of oil in the pan. Use a scant ½-cup measure to scoop batter into the hot pan, then tilt and swirl the pan to spread it out to a round about 8 inches across. If the first one is too thick, thin the batter a bit with water. Cover and reduce the heat to medium-low. Cook for 1 minute, flip the bread, cover, and cook for 1 minute more. Flip the bread, and cook for 1 minute uncovered, then flip once more, and cook for 1 minute uncovered. Slide it out onto a plate and continue with the rest of the batter.

Serve the breads warm with soup, or topped with cheese, or rolled with fillings.

HOMEMADE MULTIGRAIN BISCUIT MIX AND 15-MINUTE BISCUITS

ROLLED QUINOA, ALSO CALLED QUINOA FLAKES, is a delicious flat version of the "mother Grain." If you can't find it, use wheat germ, rolled barley, or more rolled oats. This mix is incredibly flexible and can even be made with gluten-free flours. Vegans can use soy protein powder and margarine. The biscuits are substantial, crunchy, and full of grainy flavors, perfect for dipping into the Classic Squash, Wild Rice, and Apple Soup with Sage *(page 107)*.

BISCUIT MIX

- 1 cup **whole wheat pastry flour**
- 1 cup **kamut flour** *or* **spelt flour**
- 1 cup **cornmeal**
- ½ cup **old-fashioned rolled oats, rolled rye,** *or* **rolled barley**
- ½ cup **rolled quinoa** *or* **wheat germ**
- ½ cup **nonfat powdered milk**

- 2 tablespoons **baking powder**
- ¼ cup **sugar** *or* other granular sweetener
- 2 teaspoons **salt**
- ½ cup **cold butter** *or* margarine

FOR 4 BISCUITS

- 1 cup **biscuit mix**
- ¼ cup **water,** *or* more if needed
- 1 tablespoon **milk** *(optional)*

For the biscuit mix, in a large bowl, mix the flours, cornmeal, rolled grains, milk powder, baking powder, sugar, and salt. When well combined, use a grater to shred the cold butter or margarine into the bowl, tossing with the flour to coat. Squeeze the mixture in handfuls to break up the butter or margarine into small pieces. Store in zipper-top bags in the refrigerator or freezer. *(If frozen, measure what you want to use and let it come to room temperature for an hour before proceeding.)*

To make 4 biscuits, preheat the oven to 450°F. Measure 1 cup of the mix into a large bowl. Quickly stir in ¼ cup water or enough just to moisten; don't overstir. Flatten the dough in the bottom of the bowl and cut it into 4 wedges. Transfer the biscuits to an ungreased baking pan. Brush the tops with milk *(if desired)*, and bake for 10 minutes. Serve hot.

WHOLE WHEAT PASTRY FLOUR MAKES A TENDER BISCUIT, and the luscious sweet potato and cheddar add color and flavor. This is a great companion to a hearty soup, especially the Quick Summer Veggie–Wild Rice Soup *(page 98)*. Sweet potatoes can vary in their moisture content, so you may need more or less buttermilk to make a firm dough.

SWEET POTATO–CHEDDAR BISCUITS

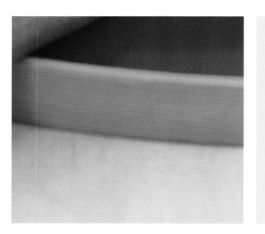

2	cups **whole wheat pastry flour**
2	teaspoons **baking powder**
1	teaspoon **baking soda**
1	teaspoon **salt**
1	tablespoon **sugar** *or* other granular sweetener
1	tablespoon **fresh herbs,** such as marjoram, thyme, *or* parsley

5	tablespoons **cold butter**
¼	cup **buttermilk,** *or* more if needed
1	cup **cooked, puréed sweet potato**
2 to 4 ounces **sharp cheddar cheese,** diced	

Preheat the oven to 400°F. Spray a nonstick baking sheet with vegetable oil spray. In a large bowl, mix the flour, baking powder, baking soda, salt, and sugar. Chop the fresh herbs and stir into the flour mixture. Grate the butter into the flour mixture and work it in with your fingers until rice-size pieces remain.

In a measuring cup, mix the buttermilk into the sweet potato. Gently stir the wet ingredients into the flour mixture, using your hands to gently knead. As it comes together, add the cheese and mix. If the dough is too dry, mix in more buttermilk, a teaspoon at a time.

Pat the dough out on a floured counter, about ¾ inch thick, and cut in either rounds or squares. Pat the scraps together to cut again. Place the biscuits on the prepared baking sheet and bake for 15 to 20 minutes, until golden and lightly browned.

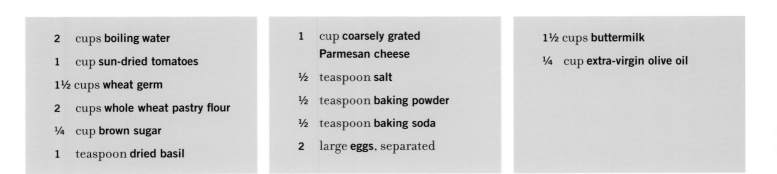

2	cups **boiling water**	1	cup **coarsely grated Parmesan cheese**	1½ cups **buttermilk**
1	cup **sun-dried tomatoes**	½	teaspoon **salt**	¼ cup **extra-virgin olive oil**
1½ cups **wheat germ**		½	teaspoon **baking powder**	
2	cups **whole wheat pastry flour**	½	teaspoon **baking soda**	
¼	cup **brown sugar**	2	large **eggs**, separated	
1	teaspoon **dried basil**			

THE GERM OF THE WHEAT KERNEL IS WHERE THE NUTRIENTS ARE STORED, so this muffin is extra-nutritious. You can substitute oat bran if you are looking for more fiber. I enjoy a savory muffin like this alongside a bowl of soup, and the Italian flavors make it a great companion to the Zuppa Fiorentina (*page 99*) or Creamy Cannellini Bean–Amaranth Soup with Basil (*page 110*).

WHEAT GERM AND SUN-DRIED TOMATO MUFFINS

Preheat the oven to 350°F. In a small, heat-safe bowl, pour the boiling water over the sun-dried tomatoes and cover with a small plate, to let them plump. When they are fully rehydrated and soft, drain them and squeeze out the excess water, then chop into ¼-inch pieces. Line a 12-cup muffin pan with paper muffin liners, and spritz the top of the pan with vegetable oil spray to keep the muffin tops from sticking.

In a large bowl, mix the wheat germ, flour, brown sugar, basil, Parmesan, salt, baking powder, and baking soda. In another bowl or measuring cup, whisk the egg yolks with the buttermilk and olive oil. Using an electric mixer, beat the egg whites to stiff peaks.

Mix the buttermilk mixture and the chopped tomatoes into the dry ingredients, then fold the egg whites into the batter. Scoop the batter into the prepared muffin cups, filling them just to the top of the cup. Bake for 20 to 25 minutes, until a toothpick inserted in the center of a muffin comes out clean. Cool on racks.

TAKE A TRIP TO THE TROPICS WITH THESE MUFFINS. They are a great example of using strong accent flavors to balance the stronger flavor of whole wheat flour. Soft whole wheat pastry flour helps keep the muffins tender while contributing the full fiber and benefits of wheat. If your limes are small, get a couple extra, so you will have enough juice.

LIME-COCONUT BANANA MUFFINS
WITH **MACADAMIAS**

Preheat the oven to 350°F. Coarsely chop the macadamia nuts and reserve. Line a 12-cup muffin pan with paper muffin liners, and spritz the top of the pan with vegetable oil spray to keep the muffin tops from sticking.

In a large bowl, mix the flour, baking soda, salt, and coconut. In a food processor or blender, purée the bananas. Add the brown sugar, and purée again. Grate the zest from the limes and add to the dry mixture, then juice the limes and measure ½ cup of the juice for the batter, reserving 2 tablespoons for the glaze. Add the ½ cup lime juice, egg, and oil to the banana mixture and purée to mix.

Stir the wet mixture into the dry mixture, then fold in the macadamias. Portion into the 12 muffin cups. Bake for 25 minutes, or until a toothpick inserted in the center of a muffin comes out clean. Cool on a rack.

When the muffins are completely cool, measure the powdered sugar, reserved 2 tablespoons lime juice, and vanilla into a shallow bowl. Stir thoroughly to make a thick paste. If it is too dry, add a few more drops of juice. Dip each cooled muffin into the glaze, gently scraping off the excess on the side of the bowl. Let the muffins dry on a cooling rack before putting them in an airtight container.

½ cup **macadamia nuts**

2 ¼ cups **whole wheat pastry flour**

1 teaspoon **baking soda**

½ teaspoon **salt**

½ cup **unsweetened coconut**, shredded

2 large, **overripe bananas**

1 cup **brown sugar**

4 **limes**

1 large **egg**

½ cup **vegetable oil**

1 cup **powdered sugar**

½ teaspoon **vanilla extract**

WHAT TO DO WITH THAT BROWN RICE LEFT OVER FROM DINNER? Make these delicious rolls, and savor the moist, chewy presence of whole grains all week. Rolls are the easiest to make and quickest to bake of all yeast breads. They freeze well and can be taken out of the freezer one at a time to thaw, for ultimate flexibility.

FAST AND **FLEXIBLE WHOLE-GRAIN ROLLS**

2	cups **water**, divided, for bulgur, *or* 1½ cups water for cooked grain
½	cup **bulgur** *or* 1 cup cooked grain
¼	cup **honey** (*not raw honey; it may kill the yeast*)
½	cup **olive oil** *or* nut oil
½	teaspoon **rice vinegar**
1	tablespoon **quick-rise yeast**
5	cups **whole wheat bread flour**, divided
2	teaspoons **salt**

Bring 1½ cups water to a boil in a small saucepan. Add the bulgur and return to a full, rolling boil. Cover, lower the heat, and simmer for 10 minutes, then let stand for 5 minutes. Add ½ cup cool water to bring the temperature down. *(If using cooked grain, bring 1½ cups water to a boil, add the cooked grain, and remove from the heat.)*

Stir the honey, oil, and vinegar into the hot grain mixture. Take the temperature of the mixture, and follow the yeast package recommendations, letting it cool if necessary. In a stand mixer or large bowl, mix 4 cups of the flour with the yeast and salt. Using the dough hook, stir in the grain mixture. Knead to mix. When the flour is mixed in, knead in the remaining cup, to make a soft dough. The dough will seem sticky in the bowl, but you should be able to handle it without it sticking to your hands. Oil a large mixing bowl and scrape the dough into the bowl. Cover tightly with plastic wrap and let rise in a warm place for at least 45 minutes, and up to 3 hours.

Oil a heavy sheet pan. Preheat the oven to 375°F. The dough should be bigger than it was. Tear off small handfuls of dough, about three-fourths of the size you would like the rolls to be. Roll each piece into a ball, and place on the oiled pan. Lightly cover with a sheet of plastic wrap. Let rise in a warm spot for at least 30 minutes.

Bake for 15 minutes. Slide the rolls off the pan onto a rack to cool.

VARIATIONS:

Add herbs, nuts, or cheese to the dough. You can make it sweeter by doubling the honey, and use it for cinnamon rolls.

After the first rising, pat the dough out to a large rectangle and cover with a filling *(see the list below)*, then roll up into a cylinder. Slice the roll in 1-inch-thick rounds, and place on the pan. Bake as directed in the main recipe.

SUGGESTED FILLINGS:

Cinnamon–sugar and raisins, shredded cheese and nuts or sautéed onions, pesto and grated Parmesan, spinach and feta, garlic and sun-dried tomatoes.

THIS SPICY LOAF IS STUDDED WITH CHEWY BARLEY AND ZINGY GINGER CHUNKS. Job's tears, if you can get it, is an outstanding grain in this bread. Purple barley is a colorful addition, as would be red or black rice. Start with a heaping $\frac{1}{3}$ cup grain to get 1 cup after cooking, and let it cool completely before adding it to the batter.

2	cups **whole wheat pastry flour**
1	cup **raw sugar** *or* brown sugar
1	teaspoon **baking powder**
1	teaspoon **baking soda**
½	teaspoon **salt**

CRYSTALLIZED GINGER AND BARLEY TEA BREAD

1	teaspoon **ground cinnamon**
¼	teaspoon **ground nutmeg**
2	large **eggs**, lightly beaten
½	cup **vegetable oil**
1	cup **buttermilk** *or* yogurt
2	teaspoons **vanilla extract**
1	cup **cooked barley** *or* **Job's tears**, cooled
1	cup **chopped crystallized ginger**
2	tablespoons **turbinado sugar**, such as Sugar in the Raw

Preheat the oven to 350°F. Spray a loaf pan with vegetable oil. In a large bowl, stir together the flour, sugar, baking powder, baking soda, salt, cinnamon, and nutmeg.

In 1-quart bowl, mix the eggs, oil, buttermilk, and vanilla. Quickly stir into the dry mixture and fold in the cooked barley and ginger. Scrape into the prepared pan and sprinkle the top with turbinado sugar.

Bake for 1 hour, until a toothpick inserted in the center of the loaf comes out clean. Cool on a rack.

WHOLE FARRO, KAMUT, OR ANY GRAIN MAKES A CHEWY, SWEET NOTE in this focaccia. Farro is an ancient variety of wheat, probably used in antiquity to make breads, risotti, and even pasta.

FARRO-STUDDED FOCACCIA WITH HERBS

¼ cup **whole farro** *or* **kamut**

1½ cups **boiling water**

3 cups **whole wheat bread flour**

2 teaspoons **quick-rise yeast**

1 teaspoon **salt**

1¼ cups **water**

5 tablespoons **extra-virgin olive oil**, divided

2 tablespoons **fresh thyme leaves**

1 tablespoon **fresh rosemary leaves**

½ small **onion**, thinly sliced

½ cup **grated Parmesan cheese**, *or* ½ teaspoon coarse salt

Cook the farro in the 1½ cups boiling water in a small saucepan for about 40 minutes, until very tender. Drain well. In a stand mixer or large bowl, mix the flour, yeast, and salt. Heat the 1¼ cups water to the temperature the yeast package recommends for mixing into a dry mixture, usually 110°F to 130°F. With the mixer running, pour in the water and 3 tablespoons of the oil. Knead until well mixed, then knead for 5 minutes more. It will be a sticky, soft dough. Knead in the cooked farro.

Grease a 9-inch square baking pan with a little olive oil. Scrape the dough into the prepared pan and spread it out to the corners. Let the focaccia rise, covered, for an hour, or until doubled in height.

Preheat the oven to 375°F. When the focaccia has risen, sprinkle the thyme, rosemary, and onion over the dough. Drizzle with the remaining olive oil, and top with the Parmesan or salt. Bake for 20 to 25 minutes, until the focaccia is firm and browned around the edges.

THE POWER BAGEL IS SOMETHING THAT APPEARED IN STORES a few years ago. As far as I can tell, the bagel's "power" lies in the fact that it actually contains fiber. These hearty buns have the darlings of the "power foods" lists: soy, flax, and blueberries for antioxidants, good fats, and protein.

POWER BUNS WITH FLAX, SOY, AND BLUEBERRIES

In a stand mixer or large bowl, mix 3 cups of the whole wheat flour with the soy flour, flax seeds, yeast, and salt. In a small saucepan, stir together the hot water, oil, and honey. Take the temperature of the mixture, and heat the mixture if necessary to adjust the temperature according to the yeast package directions. Using the dough hook or by hand, stir the liquid into the dry ingredients. Knead until the dough is well mixed, then knead for 10 minutes more. The dough can be a little sticky; add some more flour to make a supple dough, but don't add too much or the buns will be tough. Knead in the blueberries.

After kneading, scrape the dough into a large, oiled bowl. Cover the bowl with plastic wrap and set in a warm place to rise for an hour. The dough should have doubled in bulk. Oil a sheet pan. Punch down the dough, then tear off pieces, each about ½ cup in volume. Shape into rolls and place the prepared pan. Cover loosely with plastic wrap and put somewhere warm to rise for about 30 minutes. Preheat the oven to 375°F.

When the buns have almost doubled, bake them for 15 minutes. They should be golden brown and sound hollow when tapped on the bottom. Transfer the buns to a rack to cool.

3 ¼ cups	**whole wheat bread flour**, divided
½ cup	**soy flour**
¼ cup	**flax seeds**
1 tablespoon	**quick-rise yeast**
2 teaspoons	**salt**
1½ cups	**hot water**
¼ cup	**canola oil**
¼ cup	**honey**
½ cup	**dried blueberries**

RUSTIC WALNUT RAISIN BREAD

TO MAKE THE KIND OF RUSTIC BREADS YOUR FAVORITE BAKERY PRODUCES, you need patience and a few pieces of equipment. A pizza stone, water misting bottle, and pan of water for the oven are necessary to get the crisp crust. Your flour makes all the dif-ference, so try a few brands made from hard winter wheat and see how each affects the final product. This makes a dense, crusty loaf, filled with intense wheaty flavor.

1	cup **water**
4	cups plus **2** tablespoons **whole wheat bread flour**, divided
4	teaspoons **quick-rise yeast**, divided
½	cup **raisins**
1	cup **warm water**
2	tablespoons **barley malt syrup**
2	tablespoons **gluten flour**
2	teaspoons **salt**
½	cup **broken walnuts**
½	cup **sesame seeds**

continued

Four hours before mixing the dough, make the sponge. In a ceramic bowl, mix the 1 cup water, 1 cup of the flour, and 2 teaspoons of the yeast. Cover the bowl with a dampened kitchen towel and set somewhere warm to ferment for 4 hours, after which the sponge should be bubbly. At this point, you can refrigerate the sponge overnight, then let it sit for an hour to come to room temperature before mixing the dough.

Pour the sponge into a stand mixer bowl or large mixing bowl, and fit the mixer with the dough hook. Plump the raisins by soaking them in hot water, then draining. Mix the 1 cup warm water with the malt syrup and stir it into the sponge. Combine 1 cup of the remaining flour with the remaining 2 teaspoons yeast, gluten flour, and salt and mix into the sponge, then raise the speed of the mixer and beat for 2 minutes to activate the gluten. Knead the dough, adding the last 2 cups and 2 tablespoons of flour as needed to make a soft, slightly sticky dough. Knead the dough for 10 minutes. Knead in the raisins and walnuts. Oil a large mixing bowl, and transfer the dough to the bowl. Cover the bowl tightly with plastic wrap, and put it in a warm place to rise for 2 hours, or until tripled in bulk.

Spread the sesame seeds on a baking sheet with no rim or a pizza peel, having them close to one edge, so that the seeds will act like little furniture feet to slide the loaves onto the stone. Punch down the dough, and cut the mass in half. Tuck the edges under, shaping each loaf into an oval or round. Try to tuck the raisins inside, so they will not stick out and burn. Place the loves on the sesame seeds, at least 4 inches apart. Cover loosely with a damp towel and let rise for at least an hour, until the loaves are doubled in bulk.

Preheat a pizza stone for 30 minutes at 425°F. Put a small pan of water in the bottom of the oven, and have a water mister close by. When the stone is hot, use a sharp knife to slash the loaf tops quickly, then use a long metal spatula to help slide the loaves onto the stone, trying not to deflate them. Spritz with water and bake for 20 minutes, spritzing again after 5 minutes.

When the loaves sound hollow when tapped with a finger, they are done. Cool on racks completely before slicing.

CORNMEAL ADDS GREAT TEXTURE AND FLAVOR TO BREADS, as well as being as high in antioxidants as spinach. The island twist of using coconut makes this bread ever so tender and luscious, even without adding oil. Vegans can substitute a couple table-spoons of coconut milk for the egg.

JAMAICAN COCONUT CORNBREAD

1	cup **unsweetened shredded coconut**
1	cup **coarse cornmeal**
1	cup **whole wheat pastry flour**
1	tablespoon **baking powder**
½	teaspoon **salt**
¼	cup **firmly packed brown sugar**
1½	cups **coconut milk**
1	large **egg**

Preheat the oven to 300°F. Oil a 9-by-9-inch square baking pan and set aside. Spread the coconut on a rimmed baking sheet and bake for 5 minutes, then stir, bake for 5 minutes more, and stir again. When the coconut is golden, transfer to a bowl to cool. Raise the temperature of the oven to 400°F.

In a large bowl, stir together the coconut, cornmeal, pastry flour, baking powder, salt, and brown sugar. Break up any clumps of brown sugar with your fingers. In a small bowl, whisk the coconut milk and egg. Stir the wet mixture into the dry mixture and transfer to the prepared baking pan, smoothing the top of the batter. Bake for 15 minutes, or until a toothpick inserted in the center of the loaf comes out clean. Cool on a rack.

WARM WHOLE SIDES

FAST, FLEXIBLE, AND FILLING, this pilaf will help you get fiber-rich meals on the table in no time. You can use the tomato juices as part of the cooking liquid for a sprightly orange hue, and vary everything to suit your taste.

QUICK BEAN AND VEGETABLE COUSCOUS OR BULGUR PILAF

2	tablespoons **olive oil**
1	large **carrot**, shredded
1	large **onion**, chopped (*about 2 cups*)
2	cloves **garlic**, minced
1	14-ounce can **diced canned tomatoes**, drained
½	teaspoon **freshly cracked black pepper**

¾	teaspoon **salt**
1	15-ounce can **black beans,** **garbanzos,** *or* white beans, drained *and* rinsed
1¼	cups **vegetable stock** *or* water
1	cup **whole wheat couscous** *or* **bulgur**
½	cup **chopped fresh parsley**
4	ounces **aged cheese**, shredded

Heat the olive oil in a 4-quart saucepan with a tight-fitting lid. Add the carrot and onion and sauté over medium heat until soft and golden, the longer the better. Add the garlic, tomatoes, pepper, salt, and beans. Sauté, stirring gently, until everything is heated through. Add the stock or water, push the veggies to the sides, and bring the liquids to a full boil. Turn off the heat, add the couscous, stir once quickly, and cover tightly. *(If using bulgur, return to a full boil, cover tightly, simmer for 10 minutes, then take off the heat.)*

Let the pot stand, covered, at room temperature for 10 minutes to absorb the liquids and flavors. Add the parsley, fluff with a fork, and serve warm, topped with the cheese.

½ large **onion**, chopped
(about 1 cup)

1 tablespoon **chopped fresh thyme**, sage, *or* rosemary

1 tablespoon **olive oil**

2 small **carrots**, chopped

3 stalks **celery**, chopped

4 cups **chicken stock**
or other stock

½ teaspoon **salt**

½ teaspoon **freshly cracked black pepper**

½ cup **wild rice** *or* **black** *or* **red rice**, washed *and* rinsed

1½ cups **brown basmati rice** *or* other **long-grain rice**, washed *and* rinsed

½ cup **dried cranberries** *or* other dried fruit, chopped if large

½ cup **pecans** *or* other nuts, toasted

I LIKE TO THINK THAT THE INDIGENOUS PEOPLES OF NORTHERN MINNESOTA would have enjoyed this dish. Wild rice, cranberries, and some kinds of nuts were flourishing around the Great Lakes thousands of years ago. Try molding each serving in a ramekin for a restaurant-style presentation.

CLASSIC BROWN AND WILD RICE AND HERB PILAF

In a heavy-bottomed 4-quart saucepan over medium-high heat, sauté the onion and thyme in the olive oil until soft but not browned *(about 5 minutes)*. Add the carrots and celery and sauté until softened. Add the stock, salt, and pepper. Bring to a boil, and add the washed rices. Return to a boil, then lower the heat to low and simmer, covered, until the liquid is absorbed, 45 to 50 minutes.

Add the cranberries. Remove from the heat, cover, and let stand for about 5 minutes. For an elegant presentation, pack each serving into an oiled 1-cup ramekin or measuring cup and tap it out onto a small plate. Serve hot with the pecans on top.

MAKE A BATCH OF THIS TASTY DISH AND SERVE HALF WARM TONIGHT, then use the rest to stuff Whole-Grain Wraps *(see page 116)* tomorrow. Pumpkin seeds are rich in minerals and complement the already high-protein, high-mineral quinoa.

MEXICAN QUINOA WITH PEPITAS AND CILANTRO

1½ cups **water**

1 cup **quinoa**

½ cup **raw pumpkin seeds**

1 cup **cilantro leaves**, washed *and* dried

2 cloves **garlic**

½ **jalapeño chile**

½ teaspoon **salt**

1 teaspoon **ground cumin**

2 tablespoons **olive oil**

1 teaspoon **lime juice**

1 small **red bell pepper**, chopped

2 **scallions**, chopped

In a 2-quart pot with a tight-fitting lid, bring the water to a boil. In a medium bowl, rinse the quinoa with warm water, pour off most of the water, then drain in a fine-mesh strainer. When the water boils, add the quinoa and bring it back to a boil. Reduce the heat to the lowest setting, cover, and simmer for 15 minutes. The water should all be absorbed, and small holes should have formed on the surface of the grain. Let stand, covered, for 5 minutes, to finish steaming.

In a large sauté pan over high heat, dry-toast the pumpkin seeds. Shaking the pan, move the seeds over the heat until they begin to pop. Remove from the heat and put them into a food processor or blender. Add the cilantro, garlic, jalapeño, salt, and cumin and process, scraping the sides down frequently, until all the ingredients are well minced. Gradually add the olive oil and lime juice, processing until smooth.

If serving immediately, stir the cilantro mixture, bell pepper, and scallions into the quinoa while still warm. Otherwise, chill the quinoa and add the remaining ingredients when it is cool.

THE HAPPY ACCIDENT OF A BROWNED BOTTOM ON A POT OF RICE is a treasured delicacy in many cultures. In Spain, the crust on the bottom of paella is called *socorrat*, and in Iran it is called *tadeeg*. The Japanese save the *koge*, or crust, for soaking in hot tea. There are many methods for achieving crusty rice. I find the stovetop method to be very tricky, so I use a glass dish so that I can see the crust instead of guessing.

1	cup **medium-grain brown rice**, washed *and* rinsed
¼	cup **sour cream**
1	large **egg** *(optional)*
¼	teaspoon **paprika**
1	large pinch **saffron**, crumbled

½	teaspoon **ground cumin**
½	teaspoon **salt**
2	tablespoons **olive oil**
2	**new yellow potatoes**, *or* ½ small sweet potato, thinly sliced
½	cup **thinly sliced onion**

PERSIAN SPICED RICE WITH CRISPY POTATO CRUST

Preheat the oven to 400°F. Bring a large pot of water to a boil, and add the washed rice. Boil the rice for 25 minutes, then drain. In a large bowl, mix the sour cream, egg *(if using)*, paprika, saffron, cumin, and salt. Shake the rice in the strainer to release all the water, then mix the rice into the sour cream mixture.

Drizzle the olive oil over the bottom of a rounded glass 1-quart baking dish with a lid. Place the potatoes and onion in a single layer in the oil, and up the sides a bit. Put the dish in the oven for 5 minutes, then scatter the rice mixture over the potatoes, pressing it into the bottom of the dish. Cover and bake for 30 minutes. When the rice is cooked through and a brown crust is visible through the sides of the pan, use a knife or narrow spatula to loosen the edges. Place a platter or plate over the baking dish and invert the two, so that the crusty part will be on top. *(Do this over a sink; some oil may drip.)* Serve immediately, while the crust is crisp.

EVERYONE NEEDS A FEW RECIPES THAT CAN BE QUICKLY PULLED TOGETHER from pantry staples. A spicy sauce based on red peppers is a welcome change from the same old tomato sauce, and the piquancy complements the hearty whole wheat pasta. Whole wheat spaghetti has improved in the last few years, so try a few brands to see which one you like.

PANTRY PASTA "ARRABBIATA"

3	tablespoons **extra-virgin olive oil**
2	large **cloves garlic**, chopped
1	small **red onion**, chopped (*about 1 1/2 cups*)
2	tablespoons **chopped fresh flat-leaf parsley**

1/2	teaspoon **red pepper flakes**, *or* to taste
1	16-ounce jar **roasted red peppers**, drained *and* coarsely chopped
1/2	teaspoon **coarse salt**

1/2	teaspoon **freshly cracked black pepper**
3	tablespoons **capers**
8	ounces **whole wheat spaghetti**
1/2	cup **fresh basil leaves**
4	sprigs **basil**, for garnish

Bring a large pot of salted water to a boil. In a large sauté pan, heat the olive oil. Add the garlic, onion, parsley, and red pepper flakes and sauté over medium heat until very soft. Add the roasted red peppers, salt, and black pepper and continue cooking for 3 to 4 minutes, until all is tender. Purée the mixture in a food processor, then transfer it back to the pan. Keep the sauce warm and add the capers.

Cook the pasta in the boiling water according to the package directions and drain thoroughly. Add to the sauce in the pan and heat, stirring, for 30 seconds. Chop the basil leaves and add to the pasta, toss to combine, and serve, garnished with basil sprigs.

MILLET-CAULIFLOWER "MASHED POTATOES"

THIS IS AN OLD MACROBIOTIC PREPARATION, created because potatoes are a member of the nightshade family, and thus are prohibited in a macrobiotic diet. In today's world, the poor potato is avoided for its carbohydrates, so try this whole-grain and vegetable purée instead. Adding restaurant-style flavors will jazz it up, as will butter or gravy.

Wash and drain the millet, then put it in a 1-quart saucepan with a lid. Add the water, cauliflower, and salt. Bring to a boil and reduce the heat to the lowest simmer. Cover and cook for 35 minutes, checking and giving it a stir after 30 minutes. The millet will break open and thicken the liquid in the pot. When the millet is very soft and thick, take it off the heat and let stand for 5 minutes.

Use a blender for the smoothest purée, but a food processor will work almost as well. Purée until the mixture is as smooth as you can get it. Add butter or other flavorings, if desired, and serve in place of mashed potatoes.

½	cup **millet**
2 ½	cups **water**
4	ounces **sliced cauliflower stems and florets** (*about 1 ½ cups*)
½	teaspoon **salt**
	Butter, roasted garlic, wasabi, horseradish, *and/or* sour cream to taste (*optional*)

MY FAVORITE THING ABOUT THANKSGIVING when I was growing up was always the sage-laced stuffing. This hearty rendition has chewy wild rice and whole wheat bread, and apples and nuts for even more sensations as you chew. Don't wait for the holidays to make this dish; it's a great way to use up stale bread and can be made with bulgur, buckwheat, or any of the rices.

WILD RICE AND HAZELNUT STUFFING WITH APPLES

1   cup **water**

¼   cup **wild rice**

4   cups **cubed whole wheat bread** (*about 5 slices*)

2   tablespoons **butter** *or* oil

½   large **onion**, chopped (*about 1 cup*)

2   stalks **celery**, chopped

1   medium **carrot**, chopped

1   large **Granny Smith apple**, peeled, cored, *and* chopped

2   cups **vegetable stock**

½   teaspoon **freshly cracked black pepper**

1   teaspoon **dried thyme**

2   tablespoons **chopped fresh sage**

1   teaspoon **salt**

¼   cup **hazelnuts**, toasted, skins rubbed off, *and* coarsely chopped

In a small saucepan, bring the 1 cup water to a boil and cook the wild rice in it. Put the bread cubes in a large bowl and let them dry out for an hour or so, if you have time.

Preheat the oven to 400°F. In a large Dutch oven or pasta pot, heat the butter and sauté the onion, celery, and carrot over medium heat until all are tender. Add the apples, stock, pepper, herbs, and salt and bring to a simmer. Take the pot off the heat and stir in the bread cubes and cooked wild rice.

Scrape the stuffing into a 2-quart casserole or baking dish and top with the chopped hazelnuts, pressing the mixture down with the back of a spoon. You can cover and refrigerate the stuffing for up to 4 days at this point. Bake, uncovered, for about 20 minutes, until the top is golden brown.

THIS IS A GOOD DO-AHEAD DISH. The richness of the chèvre, the sweet earthiness of the shallots, and the nutty buckwheat combine to make this gratin intensely good. It may not look like much, but it melts in your mouth.

RICH AND **TANGY BUCKWHEAT** AND **CHÈVRE GRATIN**

2	tablespoons **extra-virgin olive oil**
6	large **shallots**, thinly sliced *(about 2 cups)*
½	cup **buckwheat groats**
1½	cups **chicken stock**
1	sprig **thyme** *or* rosemary
2	ounces **chèvre goat cheese** *(¼ cup)*
½	teaspoon **salt** *(optional)*
¼	cup **grated Parmesan cheese**

Heat the oil in a large sauté pan over high heat, then add the shallots. When they start to sizzle, reduce the heat to medium-low and cook, stirring often. As they soften, reduce the heat to the lowest setting, and stir every 5 minutes. Oil a medium gratin pan or 8-inch square baking dish.

In a 2-quart heavy-bottomed saucepan, heat the buckwheat over high heat. Swirl the pan to heat the grains evenly. When the groats are fragrant and hot to the touch, quickly dump them into a wire-mesh strainer, rinse, drain, and put them back in the pan. Carefully add the stock *(it will boil up when it hits the hot pan, so hold it away from you and go gradually)*. Add the thyme and bring the buckwheat mixture back to a boil. Reduce to a simmer and cook for 25 minutes. Preheat the oven to 400°F.

When the shallots are caramel colored and have cooked down, remove them from the heat. When the buckwheat is tender and all the stock is absorbed, take it off the heat. Scrape the warm buckwheat into a food processor, and pulse to coarsely purée. Add the chèvre, salt *(if using)*, and shallots, and pulse to mix. Spread the mixture in the prepared baking pan so that it is in a thin layer. Sprinkle the Parmesan over the gratin and bake for 20 minutes, until the cheese is golden.

THIS INDIAN-INSPIRED RICE DISH IS JUST AS GOOD COLD AS IT IS HOT. Brilliant red rice gets an antioxidant boost from turmeric, another brightly colored food with protective properties. If using Himalayan red rice, use 1½ cups water. Long-grain brown basmati would be in keeping with the Indian tradition.

1	tablespoon **canola oil**
	or ghee
1	tablespoon **chopped ginger**
1	tablespoon **brown mustard seeds**
½	teaspoon **chili powder**
1	teaspoon **ground turmeric**

INDIAN RED RICE PULAO WITH PISTACHIOS

1	cup **red rice** *or* **brown basmati rice**		2	cups **cauliflower florets**
2	cups **water**		½	cup **dried currants**
1	medium **carrot**, sliced		2	tablespoons **lemon juice**
2	tablespoons **brown sugar** *or* jaggery		2	large **scallions**, slivered
1	teaspoon **salt**		½	cup **shelled pistachios** *or* toasted sliced almonds

In a 2-quart pot, heat the oil briefly over medium-high heat, then add the ginger and brown mustard seeds. When the ginger is fragrant and the seeds are popping a bit, add the chili powder and turmeric and cook for a few seconds more. Add the rice, water, carrot, brown sugar, and salt and bring to a boil. Cover tightly and reduce the heat to the lowest setting. Set a timer for 35 minutes. When the timer goes off, quickly put the cauliflower and currants on top of the rice, put the lid back on, and cook for 10 more minutes.

Take the rice off the burner and let stand, covered, for 5 minutes. Fold in the lemon juice, and then serve topped with scallions and pistachios.

4   cups **vegetable stock**

½   large **onion**, chopped (*1 cup*)

2   tablespoons **olive oil**

1   cup **pearled barley**, washed *and* rinsed

½   cup **white wine**

1   pound **butternut squash**, baked *and* puréed (*1 cup*)

1   tablespoon **chopped fresh thyme**

1   teaspoon **freshly cracked black pepper**

1   teaspoon **salt**

½   cup **grated Parmesan cheese**

CREAMY WINTER SQUASH AND BARLEY RISOTTO WITH RED BELL PEPPER COULIS

PEARLED BARLEY MAKES A GREAT RISOTTO, spilling its healthful starches into a broth and never overcooking. Hulled barley needs more time and some vigorous stirring to break out the contents of the grain. Short rices and grains in the wheat family would also be delicious in this recipe. I dress it up with a brilliant red pepper coulis, which is just a fancy name for a puréed sauce. You can skip the sauce for simplicity, or serve it this way as a main dish with a round of chèvre or a few garlicky sautéed shrimp on top.

COULIS

2 medium **red bell peppers**, chopped

1 14-ounce can **diced tomatoes**, drained *and* excess liquid squeezed out

1 cup **vegetable stock**

2 teaspoons **honey**

1 teaspoon **balsamic vinegar**

½ teaspoon **dried dill**

½ teaspoon **salt**

Dash of **cayenne**

. . . . . .

6 **whole basil leaves**, for garnish

Heat the stock in a 2-quart saucepan. In a large, heavy frying pan with a lid, sauté the onion in the olive oil over medium heat, just to soften. Add the washed barley, stir to coat with oil, and keep stirring until it is hot to the touch. Add the wine and 3 cups of the simmering stock. Cover the pan and set a timer for 40 minutes. Stir occasionally and keep simmering gently. After 40 minutes, the barley should be soft and swimming in thickened stock. Add the remaining hot stock ½ cup at a time, simmering until it is absorbed. If all the stock has been absorbed and the barley is still firm or dry, add water. When the barley is creamy, add the squash, thyme, pepper, and salt. Simmer for 5 minutes, adding liquid as needed for a good consistency. Stir in the cheese, cover, and keep warm until serving.

While making the risotto, make the coulis. In a medium saucepan, bring the bell peppers, tomatoes, and 1 cup stock to a boil, then cover and reduce to a strong simmer for 10 minutes. Take the pan off the heat and let cool for a few minutes, then transfer to a blender. Put a folded towel over the lid of the blender as you purée, to prevent any hot liquids from splashing out on your hands. Purée the bell pepper mixture, then add the honey, vinegar, dill, salt, and cayenne and process to mix.

On each plate, place a cup of risotto, and ladle ½ cup of the coulis around it. Serve with a fresh basil garnish.

SUPPLÌ IN ITS ORIGINAL FORM IS A WAY TO USE UP LEFTOVER RISOTTO, and you can make it with any cooked sticky grain. For a simpler cooking process, it can be made into one large, flat cake, instead of little balls. I am lucky enough to be able to get whole wheat panko, a really crisp, large-grained breadcrumb in the Japanese style. Just use coarse, dry breadcrumbs if you can't find it.

BROWN RICE RISOTTO SUPPLÌ WITH **CREAMY SPINACH SAUCE**

RISOTTO

2 tablespoons **extra-virgin olive oil**

½ cup **minced onion**

1 cup **short-grain brown rice**

3 cups **chicken stock** or vegetable stock

½ teaspoon **salt**

½ cup **grated Parmesan cheese**

6 **sun-dried tomatoes**, softened and chopped

SAUCE

½ cup **chopped onion**

2 teaspoons **olive oil**

1 tablespoon **unbleached white flour**

1 cup **milk**

4 cups **fresh spinach**, washed and dried

½ cup **fresh basil leaves**

Salt and **freshly cracked black pepper**

1 cup **whole wheat pastry flour** or unbleached white flour

3 **eggs**, beaten

2 cups **whole wheat panko** or dry breadcrumbs

½ cup **olive oil**

To make the risotto, in a 4–quart saucepan with a tight-fitting lid, heat the olive oil. Sauté the onion over medium heat until soft and clear. Add the rice, and stir to coat thoroughly. Add 2 cups of the stock and the salt, bring to a boil, cover, and simmer for 30 minutes. Uncover, and begin stirring in more stock as needed to make a soft, sticky risotto. Keep cooking and stirring after each addition until you have a thick texture. Take the pan off the heat, add the Parmesan and tomatoes, and chill.

Prepare the sauce before frying the supplì. In a small saucepan, sauté the onion in the olive oil until the onion is soft and clear. Whisk in the flour and cook, whisking, for 2 to 3 minutes. Take the pan off the heat, and gradually whisk in the milk. Cook, whisking, until thickened. Put the spinach and basil in a food processor and mince thoroughly. Pour in the hot milk mixture and purée. Add salt and pepper to taste, then return the sauce to the pan to warm just before serving.

To assemble the supplì, form the cold risotto into balls, using 2 tablespoons for each one. Dredge them in the flour, then the egg, then the crumbs. Heat the oil in a large sauté pan until it shimmers, and fry the supplì until golden, about 3 minutes per side. Drain on paper towels, and serve hot, with the sauce.

2	small **Sweet Dumpling squash** *or* acorn squash, 6 inches *or* less in diameter
½	cup **wild rice**
1½	cups **water**
3	tablespoons **fresh sage**
½	cup **fresh parsley**
1	tablespoon **olive oil**
2	stalks **celery**, minced
½	large **onion**, chopped (*1 cup*)
1	teaspoon **dried marjoram**
1	teaspoon **freshly cracked black pepper**
	Pinch of **ground nutmeg**
1	teaspoon **salt**
¾	cup **pecan halves**

PECAN AND WILD RICE–STUFFED SQUASH

THESE TINY, ONE-SERVING SQUASHES ARE GOOD CONTAINERS for savory flavors. This classic dish is a great way to use wild rice, but buckwheat and quinoa would also be delicious. The nuts really bring out the nutty qualities in the rice.

Preheat the oven to 400°F. Oil 2 baking sheets. Cut each squashes in half from the stem to the tip. Scoop out the seeds and place cut-side down on the baking sheets. Bake for 20 to 30 minutes, or until easily pierced with a paring knife. Let cool. Reduce the oven heat to 375°F.

In a medium saucepan, cook the wild rice in the water, simmering until it is tender and starting to split. If there is any excess water, drain the rice in a strainer. Finely chop the sage and parsley. In a small sauté pan, heat the olive oil and sauté the celery, onion, and sage over medium heat until just softened. Stir in the parsley, marjoram, pepper, nutmeg, and salt, and take the pan off the heat.

When the squash halves are cool, use a spoon to scoop out the flesh, leaving a bit behind to keep the skins from tearing. In a large bowl, mash the flesh coarsely and reserve. Select 16 intact pecan halves for garnish, then use a food processor to grind the remaining pecans to powder. Add the ground pecans, the sautéed mixture, and the wild rice to the squash in the bowl and mix thoroughly. Stuff the mixture into the squash shells and top with the reserved pecan halves. Place in a casserole or baking dish large enough to hold all of the squash halves. Bake for 30 minutes, or until the tops feel firm to the touch.

MAKING GNOCCHI MAY SEEM LIKE A DAUNTING TASK, but I look at it this way: It requires no pasta-making skills, only rudimentary snake-rolling and cutting. It cooks quickly and is incredibly comforting and satisfying. You can make it casually, in all different sizes and shapes, and because it is cooked when it floats, there is no timing problem. This is a big batch—the gnocchi alone is 6 cups—so feel free to halve it.

WHOLE WHEAT POTATO GNOCCHI WITH TRUFFLE OIL AND MUSHROOMS

2	pounds **Yukon Gold potatoes**
1	teaspoon **salt**
	About 1¾ cups **whole wheat pastry flour**
¼	teaspoon **ground nutmeg**
½	cup **finely grated Parmesan cheese**
¼	cup **extra-virgin olive oil**, plus more for oiling the gnocchi

2	tablespoons **fresh sage**
8	ounces **baby portobellos** *or* wild mushrooms, sliced
4	cloves **garlic**, chopped
	Salt *and* freshly cracked **black pepper**
2	tablespoons **truffle oil**

In a medium saucepan, steam or boil the potatoes until tender, then peel them and put them through a ricer, or mash them very thoroughly while hot. You can rice them right onto the counter. Let cool completely to room temperature; do not chill.

Put a large pot of salted water on to boil.

When the potatoes are completely cool, add the 1 teaspoon salt, 1½ cups of the flour, the nutmeg, and Parmesan. Work it all together, and knead to make a pliable, soft dough. Add more flour as needed, trying to use as little as possible. If your potatoes are very moist, you may need more flour. To test your dough, pinch off a piece and form a ball, then drop it into the boiling water. If it does not dissolve, you have enough flour. Cook until it floats, and then scoop it out. Test and add more flour or salt to taste.

Divide the dough into 6 pieces, and roll each out on the counter to ¾-inch-thick snakes. Cut into ¾-inch slices and form ridges in each by pressing them across the tines of a fork, if desired. Put on a lightly floured tray.

Drop the gnocchi into the water, 12 at a time. When they rise to the surface and stay there, they are done. Fish them out with a slotted spoon or frying skimmer. Put them in a colander set over a bowl, and take to the sink. Gently drizzle warm water over them by the palmful, just to rinse off the starch. Drain and drizzle olive oil over them, then gently shake the colander in a circular motion to coat the gnocchi with oil. As you cook the remaining gnocchi, keep gently oiling them.

Chop the sage. In a large saute pan, sauté the mushrooms in ¼ cup olive oil over high heat. When they are tender, add the garlic and sage and sauté just until fragrant. Pour the finished gnocchi into the pan and swirl the pan to mix. Add salt and pepper to taste. Pour the truffle oil over it all and serve. (To freeze, assemble the finished gnocchi in a casserole and cover tightly. Thaw in the refrigerator and bake to reheat.)

COLD WHOLE SIDES

THE DARK FLAVOR OF BUCKWHEAT GIVES THIS SALAD A RANGE OF TASTES, from the deep, nutty grains to the tangy, sweet dressing. Brown and pigmented rices, wheat berries, and other grains are equally good with the miso dressing.

BUCKWHEAT AND BROCCOLI SALAD IN TANGY MISO DRESSING

1	cup **buckwheat groats**
1½	cups **water**
2	tablespoons **red miso**
1	tablespoon **canola oil**
1	tablespoon **rice vinegar**
1	tablespoon **dark sesame oil**
1	tablespoon **grated ginger**

1	clove **garlic**, minced *or* crushed
¼	teaspoon **red pepper flakes**
1	tablespoon **honey**
2	cups **broccoli florets**, blanched
½	cup **julienned carrot**
2	**scallions**, minced
½	cup **cashews**, toasted

In a small, heavy saucepan, heat the buckwheat groats over medium-high heat. Swirl the groats in the pan, toasting them until they are crackling, hot to the touch, and fragrant, about 5 minutes. In a wire-mesh strainer, wash the hot buckwheat quickly and drain thoroughly. Put the 1½ cups water in the pan and bring to a boil. Add the buckwheat, return to a boil, cover tightly, and reduce the heat to the lowest setting. Cook for about 20 minutes, until all the liquid is absorbed. Take the pan off the heat and let stand for 5 minutes, then transfer the cooked grain to a bowl, cover, and let cool to room temperature.

In a large measuring cup, whisk the miso, canola oil, and vinegar until smooth. Whisk in the sesame oil, ginger, garlic, pepper flakes, and honey. Pour the dressing over the cooled buckwheat and toss to coat.

To serve, spread the buckwheat on a platter, and top with the broccoli, carrot, and scallions. Sprinkle the cashews over the salad and serve. Alternatively, mix the veggies into the grain and chill.

AFRICAN MILLET SALAD WITH CORN AND PEPPERS

MILLET IS AN ANCIENT AFRICAN STAPLE FOOD, always served soft enough to eat with the fingers. In this recipe, you infuse the grains with spices and aromatics before cooking, for maximum flavor, and the sautéing step also helps keep the grains separate. The brilliant golden millet can be replaced with quicker-cooking whole wheat couscous, or even rice.

3	tablespoons **extra-virgin olive oil**, divided
1	medium **onion**, julienned (*about 1½ cups*)
2	tablespoons **chopped garlic**
2	tablespoons **minced ginger**
1	tablespoon **paprika**
1	teaspoon **ground black pepper**

⅛	teaspoon **ground allspice**
⅛	teaspoon **cayenne**, *or* to taste
1	cup **millet**
1½	cups **water**
1	teaspoon **salt**
¼	cup **lemon juice**
1	tablespoon **brown sugar**

1	8-ounce can "extra crunchy" **corn**, drained
1	small **green bell pepper**, chopped
1	whole **Roma tomato**, chopped
¼	cup **chopped fresh parsley**
¼	cup **roasted peanuts**, chopped

In a 2-quart saucepan, with a tight-fitting lid, heat 1 tablespoon of the olive oil, then sauté the onion over medium heat until very golden and soft. Add the garlic and ginger and cook for a minute, then add the paprika, black pepper, allspice, and cayenne and cook for a minute more. Wash the millet quickly and drain. Add the millet to the pan and stir, coating the grains and cooking until hot to the touch. Add the water and salt and bring to a boil, then reduce the heat and cover. Simmer on low for 20 minutes before checking for doneness. When all the liquid is absorbed and the grain is tender, cover and take the pan off the heat for 10 minutes to steam. Scrape the cooked millet into a bowl and cover, then let cool.

Whisk the remaining 2 tablespoons olive oil with the lemon juice and brown sugar in a small bowl. Stir the corn, bell pepper, tomato, and parsley into the cooled millet mixture, then drizzle the dressing over it and stir to coat. Serve topped with the peanuts.

10	ounces **Chinese-style extra firm tofu**, drained *and* pressed	2	tablespoons **dark sesame oil**	¼	teaspoon **cayenne** *(optional)*
1	bunch **asparagus**	2	tablespoons **soy sauce**	1	tablespoon **canola oil**
8	ounces **soba noodles**	2	tablespoons **minced ginger**	¼	cup **maple syrup**
2	cups **watercress leaves**, washed *and* dried	1½	teaspoons **salt**, divided	4	large **scallions**, slivered
		½	teaspoon **freshly cracked black pepper**		

SLEEK BUCKWHEAT NOODLES IN SAVORY SESAME DRESSING with peppery watercress make a bed for sweet and spicy tofu squares. This cold pasta is perfect served in rustic noodle bowls with chopsticks. Look for 100 percent buckwheat soba, as many brands are mostly refined wheat. All-buckwheat soba is trickier and more expensive to make, and more delicate to cook, but the flavor and nutrition are worth seeking out.

CHILLED SOBA WITH CRISPY SWEET TOFU AND WATERCRESS

Drain the tofu, wrap it in a kitchen towel, and place a cutting board on top to press out the water. Put a heavy pot on the board as a weight. Bring a large pot of water to a boil.

Slice about 2 inches off the tips of the asparagus, then cut the tender middle part of the stems into ½-inch pieces. Cook the soba according to the package directions, adding the asparagus tips and pieces to the pot for the last 2 minutes of cooking time. Rinse with cold water and drain thoroughly, then put in a medium bowl. Add the watercress leaves. In a small bowl, whisk the sesame oil, soy sauce, ginger, ½ teaspoon of the salt, and the pepper and toss with the soba and asparagus. Chill.

Cut the tofu into ½-inch slices, then cut them in half. Lay them on a plate and sprinkle with the remaining 1 teaspoon salt and the cayenne *(if using)*. In a large sauté pan, heat the canola oil and maple syrup over medium-high heat until the mixture starts to bubble. Carefully place the tofu slices into the bubbling syrup. Cook for 3 minutes, then flip and cook for 3 minutes more. Use your spatula to scoop the maple glaze over the tofu as it cooks. When the tofu is golden brown and most of the liquid is absorbed, lift the tofu out of the pan, leaving the oil behind.

Serve 1 cup noodles topped with one-fourth of the hot tofu, and scatter the scallions on top.

SZECHUAN CHICKEN AND RED RICE SALAD WITH SESAME DRESSING

THE CLASSIC NOODLE SALAD IS WAY BETTER MADE WITH WHOLE-GRAIN RICE. If you can get Szechuan peppercorns for this salad, crush them fresh for their unique, tongue-tingling flavor. Use the smaller measure of water for Himalayan red rice, and the larger for Wehani or other longer, larger-grain red rice.

1¾ to 2 cups **water**

1 cup **red rice**, washed *and* rinsed

3 tablespoons **tahini**

¼ cup **soy sauce**

1 tablespoon **rice vinegar**

1 tablespoon **hot sesame oil**

1 tablespoon **dark sesame oil**

1 tablespoon **sugar**

1 tablespoon **minced ginger**

2 teaspoons **minced garlic**

½ teaspoon **salt**

½ teaspoon **crushed Szechuan peppercorns** *(optional)*

8 ounces **boneless, skinless chicken breast halves**, cooked *and* shredded

2 cups **bean sprouts**

1 medium **cucumber**, peeled, seeded, *and* sliced

4 **scallions**, slivered

¼ cup **chopped dry-roasted peanuts**

In a 1-quart saucepan with a tight-fitting lid, bring the water to a boil, and add the washed rice. Return to a boil, then reduce the heat to a low simmer. Cover tightly, and cook for 25 minutes, or until the water is all absorbed. Take the pan off the heat and let stand for 10 minutes. Let the rice cool to room temperature.

In a measuring cup or small bowl, whisk the tahini, soy sauce, rice vinegar, sesame oils, sugar, ginger, garlic, salt, and crushed Szechuan pepper *(if using)*. Put the shredded chicken in a small bowl and measure 2 tablespoons of the sesame mixture over it. Toss to mix. Stir the remaining sesame mixture into the chilled rice.

On a platter, spread the rice, then top with the chicken, sprouts, and cucumber slices. Scatter the scallions and peanuts over it all and serve.

WHEAT, LIKE RICE, HAS DIFFERENT VARIETIES with differing starch balances. The first cultivated wheat, called einkorn, is ten thousand years old and still grown today. It crossbred with a wild grass to create emmer (*or farro*) and durum wheats. A few thousand more years passed before another chance crossbreeding created today's common bread wheat, as well as spelt and club wheat. If you can't get farro or spelt berries, whole hard winter wheat berries will work, as will hulled barley or whole oats.

CRUNCHY FARRO SALAD WITH ARTICHOKES, RED BELL PEPPERS AND EDAMAME

1	cup **farro** *or* **wheat berries**
2 ½	cups **vegetable stock**
1	sprig **rosemary**
½	teaspoon plus a pinch of **salt**, divided, *or* to taste
2	cloves **garlic**, peeled
2	ounces **fresh basil** (*1 ½ cups leaves*)

In a small, heavy saucepan, dry-toast the farro over high heat until hot and lightly fragrant. Add the vegetable stock, rosemary, and a pinch of salt. Bring to a boil, reduce the heat to a simmer, and cover. Cook for about an hour, until tender. Drain any excess stock and cool to room temperature.

Put the garlic, basil, and pine nuts in the work bowl of a food processor and process to chop very finely. Add the remaining ½ teaspoon salt and lemon juice and process until smooth. Gradually add the olive oil to make a smooth paste.

Trim and halve the baby artichokes and put in a large bowl of cold water with half of the lemon. Bring a large pot of water to a boil, drain the artichokes, and boil them until a knife inserted into an artichoke enters easily.

In a serving bowl, toss the cooked grain, dressing, artichokes, bell pepper, and edamame. Crack black pepper over the salad and serve.

¼ cup **pine nuts**

2 tablespoons **lemon juice**

¼ cup **extra-virgin olive oil**

12 **baby artichokes** *or* one 13-ounce jar artichoke bottoms, drained

½ **large lemon** (*if using fresh artichokes*)

1 small **red bell pepper**, sliced

1 cup **shelled edamame**, thawed

Freshly cracked black pepper

87

INDONESIAN RED RICE SALAD WITH BOILED EGGS
AND MACADAMIAS

INDONESIAN CUISINE IS A RIOT OF FLAVORS, with rice. I like the sweetness of one of the red rices here, but any brown rice will also be delicious. Himalayan red rice takes less water, so use the smaller measure if using it, while the other red rices need more liquid.

1¾ cups to 2 cups **water**

1   cup **red rice**

2   tablespoons **canola oil**

4   large **shallots**, chopped

3   cloves **garlic**, chopped

1   large **red chile**, seeded *and* chopped

1-inch piece **ginger root**, chopped

1   teaspoon **ground coriander**

1   large **carrot**, thinly sliced

8   ounces **green beans**, trimmed *and* chopped

½   cup **coconut milk**

¼   cup **soy sauce**

½   teaspoon **molasses**

4   large **eggs**, boiled *and* peeled

1   large **lime**, quartered

½   cup **julienned fresh basil**

¼   cup **macadamia nuts**, toasted *and* chopped

In a 1-quart saucepan with a tight-fitting lid, bring the water to a boil. Rinse the rice and drain in a fine-mesh strainer. Add the drained rice to the boiling water and keep the heat high until it returns to a boil. Reduce the heat to low and cook for 45 minutes, or until the water is absorbed. Let the pot stand, covered, for at least 10 minutes, and then let cool to room temperature.

In a wok or large sauté pan, heat the oil over high heat. Add the shallots, garlic, chile, ginger, coriander, carrot, and green beans. Stir-fry until the vegetables are crisp-tender.

Add the coconut milk, soy sauce, and molasses to the wok, and bring to a boil. Push the vegetables over to one side to make room for the eggs. Halve the eggs lengthwise, and place in the pan, cut–sides down. Simmer for 2 minutes. In a large bowl, mix the contents of the pan with the rice. Add the basil and macadamias, then toss and serve.

A BEAUTIFUL PRESENTATION WILL ELEVATE YOUR MEAL TO FINE DINING, and a marinated grain salad is as fine as anything out there. This is just a beginning from which to get creative. Whatever is fresh and in season simply needs an artful approach to look nice in a composed salad. Blanched asparagus, snow peas, avocado, or jicama sticks can liven up the plate.

COMPOSED SALAD OF GRAINS WITH HAZELNUT VINAIGRETTE

1	cup **barley, red rice,** *or* **kamut**
½	cup **hazelnuts**
½	cup **chopped fresh parsley**
3	cloves **garlic**
½	teaspoon **salt**
6	tablespoons **balsamic vinegar**
1	teaspoon **dried tarragon**
¾	cup **extra-virgin olive oil**
1	large **Roma tomato**
1	small **yellow squash**
4	cups **salad spinach**, washed *and* dried
1	large **carrot**, julienned
1	large **red bell pepper**, roasted *and* slivered
1	3.5-ounce package **enoki mushrooms**, *or* 1 bunch asparagus, blanched

Cook the grain until tender, then drain and let cool.

Preheat the oven to 350°F. Place the hazelnuts in a small baking pan or pie plate and toast in the oven for 10 minutes. Put the warm nuts in a kitchen towel and rub them to remove the skins. Put the cleaned nuts into a food processor. Pulse on and off to coarsely chop the hazelnuts. Remove half of the coarse chunks and reserve. Grind the remaining nuts finely, then add the parsley, garlic, and salt and grind them, too. Add the vinegar and tarragon and process, then drizzle in the oil with the motor running. Stir ½ cup of the dressing into the cooked grain.

Cut the tomato in half vertically and scrape out the seeds, then slice in vertical spears. Use a channel knife or paring knife to slice shallow, lengthwise grooves in the yellow squash, and then slice thinly.

To compose the salad on a large platter, spread the spinach to the edges of the platter, then mound the cooled grain in the center, leaving some spinach exposed at the edge. Arrange the carrot julienne on the grain in four fanned groupings, evenly spaced around the edges. Arrange the squash between the grouped carrots. Place the bell pepper slivers across the top of the mound of grain, then arrange the mushrooms and tomato spears atop that. To compose on individual plates, place the grains to one side, and group the vegetables around the plate. Drizzle the remaining dressing over the salad and top with the reserved hazelnuts.

BEAUTIFUL BLACK RICE, OR ANY OF THE RICES, MAKES A GORGEOUS BED for lemon-infused grilled veggies. The greens and veggies supplement the mineral and vitamin content of the grain, as well as providing flavor and brilliant color. For a main course, just grill some chicken or sprinkle on some feta cheese.

SUMMER GRILLED VEGETABLE SALAD WITH **BLACK RICE** AND **ARUGULA**

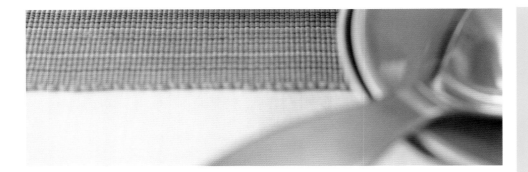

1	small **red bell pepper**
1	small **zucchini**
4	ounces **button mushrooms** *or* portobellos
4	tablespoons **extra-virgin olive oil**, divided
	Grated **zest** *and* **juice** of 1 large **lemon**
	Coarse salt (*optional*)
1	large clove **garlic**
½	cup **fresh basil leaves**
½	teaspoon **salt**

Preheat the grill, and soak 2 cups of mesquite or apple-wood chips, if desired. To smoke the vegetables in a gas grill, you will need to place the soaked chips in a smoker pan or in a packet made of foil that is open on the top and can be placed in the bottom of your grill. For a charcoal grill, build the fire on one side of the grill, and when it is time to cook, sprinkle the chips over the white ash-covered coals. You can use a grill wok or the grate to cook the vegetables.

Cut the bell pepper and zucchini in long, ½-inch-wide strips, and halve the button mushrooms if large (or cut the portobellos in ½-inch slices). Toss with 1 tablespoon of the olive oil and the lemon zest and juice. When the grill is hot, drain the wood chips and put them in your grill. Cover the grill and wait for a bit of smoke to start. Put the wok on with the veggies, or place the strips across the grate. If using a gas grill, place the veggies on the side above the chips, and lower the heat. If using a charcoal grill, put them on the side away from the pile of coals. Close the grill and let the vegetables smoke-roast for 5 minutes. Open the grill and stir or turn the vegetables until they are tender and browned.

Take the vegetables off the grill, transfer to a large bowl, and sprinkle with coarse salt to taste, if desired. Let cool. Drop the garlic into a food processor or blender with the motor running. When it is minced, add the basil and purée, scraping down to get a fine mince. Add the ½ teaspoon salt and the balsamic vinegar and purée, then gradually drizzle in the remaining 3 tablespoons oil with the motor running.

Mix half of the dressing into the cooked black rice. Spread the arugula on a large platter, drizzle the remaining dressing over it, and mound the rice in the center. Top with the grilled veggies. Crack pepper over it all and serve.

2   tablespoons **balsamic vinegar**

½   cup **black rice**, cooked in **1** cup **water** *and* cooled

2   ounces **baby arugula**, washed *and* dried

Freshly cracked black pepper

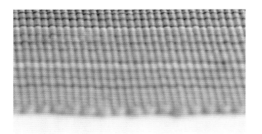

THE THOUGHT OF USING NOODLES IN A SUSHI RECIPE sounds like some kind of crazy fusion, but it's actually quite traditional. Soba is another revered food in Japan, and one thing must have led to another. These rolls are surprisingly wonderful, and the soba seems much lighter and airier in the roll than tightly packed rice.

SOBA ROLLS WITH HAZELNUTS AND BLACK SESAME SAUCE

SAUCE

⅓ cup **black sesame seeds**
(*or brown, or tahini in a pinch*)

1 tablespoon **mirin**

3 tablespoons **soy sauce**

1 tablespoon **red miso**

1 tablespoon **sugar**

½ teaspoon **hot sesame oil**

1 tablespoon **dark sesame oil**

1 tablespoon **rice vinegar**

1 clove **garlic**, crushed

ROLLS

10 ounces **salad spinach**

8 ounces **soba noodles**

4 sheets **nori**

12 large **hazelnuts**, toasted *and* skinned

½ large **carrot**, cut into long, thin strips

Mayonnaise in a squirt bottle

· · · · · ·

Pickled ginger, for serving

Wasabi, for serving

Make the sauce first. In a small sauté pan, toast the sesame seeds over medium-high heat, even if they are already toasted, just to refresh the flavor and bring out the oil. Shake the pan until the seeds are hot and fragrant. Transfer the hot seeds to a coffee grinder or spice mill, and grind them as finely as possible. Gradually add the mirin and soy sauce to the seeds and grind some more, until a smooth paste is obtained. Scrape the mixture out into a small bowl and stir in the miso, sugar, hot and dark sesame oils, rice vinegar, and crushed garlic. Cover tightly and reserve.

Wrap a rolling mat with plastic wrap, and bring a large pot of water to a boil for the spinach. Bring a second large pot of water to a boil for the soba. Drop the spinach in for 1 to 2 minutes, drain, and squeeze out. Roll in a towel to dry thoroughly. Cook the soba according to the package instructions, about 4 minutes. Drain well, rinse with warm water, and drain again. Place the soba on a double thickness of kitchen towels.

For each roll, place a sheet of nori on the rolling mat, shiny-side down. Grab about one-fourth of the noodles and drape them across the nori, leaving ½ inch of nori exposed at the top, then arrange the noodles with your fingers as evenly as possible. Sprinkle some hazelnuts in the spaces between noodles. Divide the spinach into 4 portions. Make a row of spinach on the soba, then lay a couple of carrot strips alongside the spinach. Squirt a line of mayonnaise next to the carrot. Roll up from the bottom, using your mat to keep the roll tight. Dampen the exposed nori at the top and use it to seal the roll. Let stand, seam-side down, for a minute before slicing each roll into 6 pieces.

Serve with the black sesame sauce, ginger, and wasabi.

WHOLE SOUPS AND DUMPLINGS

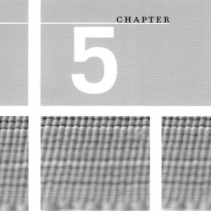

WHEN YOU HAVE A FULL VEGGIE DRAWER, MAKE SOUP. Hand-harvested Mahnomen wild rice is quicker to cook than hulled barley or wheat berries, so adjust the cooking time accordingly.

QUICK SUMMER VEGGIE–WILD RICE SOUP

3	medium **leeks**, white part only, thinly sliced
1	medium **carrot**, chopped
1	tablespoon **olive oil**
8	cups **vegetable stock**
½	cup **wild rice** *or* **barley**
1	cup **green beans**, sliced in ½-inch lengths

1	14-ounce can **chopped tomatoes**, with liquid
1	cup **sliced snow peas**
¼	teaspoon **cracked black pepper**, plus more to taste
1	tablespoon **chopped fresh thyme**
1	teaspoon **honey**

2	tablespoons **chopped fresh basil**
2	tablespoons **minced parsley**
	Salt
	Grated Parmesan cheese, for serving

In a heavy stockpot over medium-high heat, sauté the leeks and carrot in the olive oil until soft. Add the stock and wild rice and bring to a boil, then cover and reduce the heat to a simmer. Cook for 30 minutes.

When the grain is tender, add the beans, tomatoes, snow peas, ¼ teaspoon pepper, and thyme, and continue to cook for 8 minutes.

Stir in the honey, basil, and parsley and seasoning, adding salt and pepper to taste. Serve hot, garnished with a spoonful of Parmesan.

ZUPPA FIORENTINA

IN THE DELI WHERE I ONCE COOKED, SPINACH WAS THE "MAGIC INGREDIENT," because putting it in a dish like this guaranteed that it would fly out the door. This light, bright soup is named for Florence, Italy, where spinach is also popular, but it is even better with whole grains instead of white rice.

8	large **shallots** or 1 large onion, chopped (*2 cups*)
2	tablespoons **extra-virgin olive oil**
3	cloves **garlic**, chopped
1	sprig **rosemary**

2	large **bay leaves**
6	cups **chicken stock** or vegetable stock
½	cup **quinoa, barley,** or **short-grain brown rice**
1	large **carrot**, chopped

5	ounces **salad spinach** leaves, chopped
	Salt *and* **freshly cracked black pepper**
	Grated Parmesan cheese for serving (*optional*)

In a large Dutch oven or soup pot, sauté the shallots in the olive oil, starting out at medium-high heat and lowering the heat once the shallots have softened. The longer you sauté them, the better the flavor will be—20 minutes to an hour is best. You want them to turn a caramel brown and shrink to half their original volume. Add the garlic and sauté for just a couple of minutes longer. Add the rosemary, bay leaves, stock, grain, and carrot and bring to a boil. Cover, reduce the heat to a simmer, and cook for the recommended amount of time for the grain you have chosen.

When the grain is tender, remove the bay leaves, stir the spinach into the hot soup, season to taste with salt and pepper, and serve in bowls, topped with Parmesan, if desired.

THIS PREPARATION ELEVATES THE STEW TO A FINE DINING EXPERIENCE. Searing tender steak pieces and then removing them allows the *fond* of brown bits in the pan to infuse the dish and simmer into a long-cooking grain without overcooking the meat. Spinach adds a note of freshness and color. Purple or black barley, or any grain, would work well here.

FILET MIGNON AND **BARLEY "STEW"** WITH **SPINACH**

Cut the beef into 1-inch, bite-size pieces. Combine the flour, salt, and cracked pepper on a plate, and roll half of the beef in this seasoned flour. In a large Dutch oven or soup pot, heat the olive oil. Add the unfloured half of the beef, and cook over medium-high heat until the beef is browned but still rare in the center. Scrape the beef into a bowl, drain the fat back into the pan, and cook the floured beef. Transfer that beef to the bowl also. Quickly add the onion and carrot to the hot pan and scrape up the browned bits. As soon as the onion is golden, add the tomato paste and cook, stirring constantly, for 2 to 3 minutes, until it is a shade darker. Add the barley, stock, and thyme and bring to a boil. Cover, lower the heat to a simmer, and cook for 30 to 40 minutes.

When the barley is tender, add the beef to the pan and reheat. Stir in the spinach. Serve as soon as the spinach is just wilted and the beef is hot.

1	pound **beef tenderloin** *or* other tender steak
3	tablespoons **whole wheat pastry flour**
¼	teaspoon **salt**
	Freshly cracked black pepper
2	tablespoons **extra-virgin olive oil**
1	medium **onion**, chopped (*1½ cups*)
1	medium **carrot**, chopped
3	tablespoons **tomato paste**
½	cup **hulled barley**, soaked overnight
5	cups **beef stock**
1	tablespoon **chopped fresh thyme**
4	cups **coarsely chopped spinach**

WHOLE SOUPS AND DUMPLINGS

LEGUMES AND WHOLE GRAINS ARE THE COMPLEMENTARY PROTEIN FOODS that form the basis of meatless meals all over the world. Quinoa gives this bright yellow soup a nutty complexity, and the germ of the grains form tiny haloes. All the spices in this soup have great health benefits, especially the turmeric. You can always add more vegetables, like cauliflower or bell peppers, and freeze the dal for another day.

SPICY YELLOW SPLIT PEA QUINOA DAL

1	tablespoon **ghee** *or* oil
1	large **onion**, diced *(about 2 cups)*
1	tablespoon **black mustard seeds**
2	tablespoons **minced ginger**
	Minced jalapeño to taste

1	tablespoon **ground cumin**
1	teaspoon **ground turmeric**
1	tablespoon **ground coriander**
1½	cups **yellow split peas**, picked over *and* rinsed
¾	cup **quinoa**, rinsed
	About **8 cups water**, divided

2	**carrots**, chopped
1	tablespoon **raw sugar**
2	tablespoons **lemon juice**, *or* to taste
	Cayenne *(optional)*
1	teaspoon **salt**

In a 4-quart soup pot, heat the ghee. Add the onion and sauté over medium heat until softened and golden. Add the mustard seeds and sauté until fragrant, about a minute. Add the ginger, jalapeño, cumin, turmeric, and coriander and stir for another minute. Add the split peas, quinoa, and 6 cups of the water and bring to a boil.

When the peas come to a boil, add the carrots to the pot. When it boils again reduce the heat to a simmer and cover, stirring every 10 minutes and adding more water as needed, until the peas are falling apart, just under an hour.

Season the dal with the raw sugar, lemon juice, cayenne to taste *(if using)*, and salt. Purée if you want a smooth texture. Serve with hot flatbreads.

GOLDEN MILLET GIVES THIS GREEN SOUP AN EXTRA RADIANCE, as well as thickening it beautifully. Millet's softer texture allows it to disappear into the purée, while adding all the benefits of whole grain.

CREAM OF **ASPARAGUS, SORREL,** AND **MILLET SOUP** WITH **ALMONDS**

Trim the hard bottoms from the asparagus, then cut off the tips in bite-size pieces; reserve. Chop the remaining stems.

In a soup pot, sauté the onion in the olive oil over medium heat until tender and clear. Add the chopped asparagus stems (not the tips), millet, and stock. Simmer for 25 minutes, until the millet is very soft.

Steam or blanch the asparagus tips until just crisp-tender, and reserve.

Use a wire-mesh strainer over a bowl to strain the contents of the pot. Save the drained liquid. By puréeing only the solids, you will get a smoother result. Purée the millet-asparagus mixture and, when smooth, add the sorrel and purée again. Pour the milk in with the motor running, then add the reserved cooking liquid. Return to the pan and add salt and pepper to taste. Ladle a quarter of the soup into each bowl. Garnish each serving by arranging the asparagus tips in the center of the bowl, and sprinkle a tablespoon of almonds around them.

2	pounds **asparagus**
1	large **onion**, chopped (*2 cups*)
1	tablespoon **extra-virgin olive oil**
½	cup **millet**, washed *and* drained
3	cups **vegetable stock**
1	cup **fresh sorrel**, stemmed *and* sliced
1	cup **whole milk**
	Salt *and* **freshly cracked black pepper**
¼	cup **sliced almonds**, toasted

THE CLASSIC ONE-POT MEAL, WITH RICH STEW and tender dumplings, need not be an all-day affair. Boxed stock and fast biscuit-style dumplings will have this on the table in under an hour. Made with whole wheat pastry flour, the comforting dumplings will quietly nourish your body and soul. You can replace up to one-fourth of the flour with another grain flour, like teff or quinoa, for variety.

FAST CREAMY CHICKEN STEW WITH **PARSLEYED DUMPLINGS**

3	teaspoons **extra-virgin olive oil**, divided
½	large **onion**, chopped (*1 cup*)
2	stalks **celery**, chopped
1	large **carrot**, chopped
8	ounces **boneless, skinless chicken thighs**, cut into large chunks

2	cups **chicken stock**
½	teaspoon **dried thyme**
½	teaspoon **dried marjoram**
¼	cup **heavy cream**
½	cup **frozen peas** *or* edamame
½	teaspoon **salt**
½	teaspoon **freshly cracked black pepper**

continued

DUMPLINGS

1   cup **whole wheat pastry flour**

1   cup **minced fresh parsley**

½   teaspoon **baking powder**

½   teaspoon **baking soda**

½   teaspoon **salt**

1   large **egg**

6   tablespoons **yogurt**
    or buttermilk, *or* more
    as needed

In a large soup pot or Dutch oven, heat 2 teaspoons of the oil and sauté the onion, celery, and carrot over medium heat until softened. Scrape them to one side, add the remaining teaspoon of oil to the open space, and add the chicken. Sear the chicken chunks, undisturbed, over medium-high heat for a minute, and then stir. When the chicken is browned all over, add the stock, thyme, marjoram, and cream. Bring to a boil, then reduce the heat and simmer until the stew is the desired thickness. Add the peas, salt, and pepper. Keep simmering on low heat.

For the dumplings, in a large bowl, mix the flour, parsley, baking powder, baking soda, and salt. Stir in the egg and yogurt, and quickly mix. It should be a soft dough; if it is stiff, add more yogurt. Drop the dough by heaping tablespoons onto the simmering soup. Turn the heat up to medium-high, cover, and cook for 5 to 7 minutes. Uncover and cut one of the last dumplings you added in half. It should be cooked through. If it is still doughy in the center, cover and simmer for 3 to 5 minutes more.

Serve immediately.

WILD RICE OR ANY OF THE HEARTY RICES will provide a textural counterpoint to the smooth, sweet squash. Unbleached white flour works best for this, as a whole wheat roux would be less smooth.

CLASSIC SQUASH, WILD RICE, AND **APPLE SOUP** WITH **SAGE**

2-pound **butternut squash**
(*2 cups puréed*)

½   cup **wild rice**

1½ cups **water**

1   tablespoon **butter** *or* olive oil

1   large **onion**, chopped
(*2 cups*)

2   tablespoons **minced fresh sage**

4   stalks **celery**, chopped

2   tablespoons **unbleached white flour**

3   cups **whole milk**

½   teaspoon **dried thyme**

Dash of **cayenne**

½   teaspoon **salt**, *or* to taste

1   medium **Granny Smith apple**, cored *and* diced

Preheat the oven to 400°F. Oil a large baking sheet. Cut the squash in half, scoop out the seeds, and put the squash halves, cut-side down, on the baking sheet. Bake until very tender, about 30 minutes. Let the squash cool to room temperature, then purée in a food processor or blender. Measure 2 cups of purée and save any extra for another use. Cook the wild rice in the water for 20 minutes to an hour, depending on the variety. Drain off any excess water when the grains are tender.

In a soup pot, heat the butter, then sauté the onion, sage, and celery over medium heat until tender. Sprinkle in the flour and cook, stirring and scraping the bottom of the pan to prevent scorching, for about 3 minutes. Whisk in the milk, a little at a time, and bring to a simmer. Reduce the heat so the mixture just bubbles gently for a couple of minutes.

Whisk in the puréed squash, and stir over low heat. Add the thyme, cayenne, salt, wild rice, and apple, stirring over low heat just until warmed through.

BUCKWHEAT MUSHROOM KREPLACH IN **DILL TOMATO SAUCE**

THE SMALL DUMPLINGS KNOWN AS KREPLACH can be served with a sauce, as they are here, or simply floated in broth, for a light meal. Traditional Russian kasha is usually sautéed and coated with an egg before adding the water, a technique that adds a toasted flavor and keeps the grains separate. This is a gussied-up version of a simpler kreplach that is made with handmade dough.

SAUCE

- 2 tablespoons **butter**
- 1 cup **minced onion**
- 1 stalk **celery**, finely chopped
- 2 cups **tomato sauce**
- ¼ cup **white wine**
  Salt *and* **freshly cracked black pepper**
- 2 tablespoons **chopped fresh dill**

KREPLACH

- 1 tablespoon **extra-virgin olive oil**
- 2 ounces **fresh shiitake mushrooms**, minced
- ½ cup **buckwheat groats**
- 1 clove **garlic**, chopped
- 1 large **egg**
- 1 cup **water**

- ½ teaspoon **salt**, plus more to taste
- 1 teaspoon **coarsely ground black pepper**
- 2 ounces **chèvre goat cheese**
- 40 round **gyoza wrappers**

Make the sauce. Heat the butter in a 2-quart saucepan, then add the onion and celery. Cook over medium heat until softened and starting to turn golden. Add the tomato sauce and wine and simmer for 5 minutes. Add salt and pepper to taste and keep warm, adding the dill just before serving.

For the kreplach, in a 1-quart saucepan, heat the olive oil. Sauté the mushrooms over medium heat until browned and shrunken. Add the buckwheat and cook, stirring, until fragrant. Add the garlic and egg and cook, stirring, until the grains are dry and separate. Add the water, salt, and pepper, bring to a boil, then cover and reduce the heat to low. Cook for 25 minutes. Take the pan off the heat, stir in the chèvre, and let cool.

Line a sheet pan with parchment or a silicone liner for the assembled kreplach. On a cutting board, lay out several gyoza wrappers. Measure a heaping tablespoonful of the buckwheat filling onto each. Using a pastry brush, brush water around the filling, and top with another skin. Press together from the filling outward to make sure there is no air trapped inside. Place the kreplach on the sheet pan, not touching. Repeat with the remaining gyoza wrappers and filling. These can be covered tightly and refrigerated for up to 8 hours.

Bring a pot of water to a boil. Drop in 6 kreplach at a time, and when they start bobbing around on the surface, cook for 3 minutes. Scoop them out with a spider or slotted spoon. Place on an oiled serving platter or casserole as you go, and drizzle a little oil on them to prevent sticking. Reheat the tomato sauce, stir in the dill, and heat for a few minutes to wilt the herb slightly. Pour over the kreplach and serve hot.

WHOLE SOUPS AND DUMPLINGS

HERE IS A CREAMY SOUP IN WHICH NUTRIENT-DENSE AMARANTH acts as the binder. Because of amaranth's tendency to thicken, it is perfect in creamy soups. The flavors are Italian, but you can use other bean and grain combinations.

CREAMY CANNELLINI BEAN–AMARANTH SOUP WITH BASIL

2	large **leeks**, white parts only, sliced	1	cup **tomato purée**	
2	tablespoons **extra-virgin olive oil**	1	15-ounce can **cannellini beans** or white beans, drained, divided	
3	cloves **garlic**, minced	½	cup **chopped fresh basil**	
½	cup **amaranth**	2	tablespoons **chopped fresh oregano**	
2	cups **vegetable stock** or chicken stock	1	teaspoon **salt**	
1	**bay leaf**		**Freshly cracked black pepper**	

Cut the root end from the leeks and slice them in half vertically, then rinse thoroughly to remove all grit. Slice the leeks and sauté in the olive oil over medium heat in a 2-quart saucepan. When the leeks are golden and soft, add the garlic and cook for a minute, then add the amaranth, stock, bay leaf, and tomato purée, and bring to a boil. Reduce the heat to a simmer, cover, and cook for 30 minutes.

Put half of the beans into a food processor bowl. Purée until smooth. When the amaranth mixture is done, remove the bay leaf, then carefully pour the mixture into the processor and purée. Cover the top of the feed tube with a folded towel as you process, to keep hot liquid from flying out. Pour the purée back into the pan.

Stir the remaining beans and the chopped herbs into the hot soup, and warm gently on the stove for 5 minutes or so. If desired, thin with water or more stock. Season with the salt and pepper to taste. Serve hot with whole-grain bread.

WHOLE ENTRÉES

CHAPTER

6

114   Leftover Grain Scramble *with* Cheese

115   Pizzoccheri *(Italian Buckwheat Noodle Casserole)*

116   Whole-Grain Wraps *with* Quinoa, Beans, *and* Roasted Veggies

118   Middle Eastern Lentil Rice Rolls *with* Taratoor Sauce

120   Amaranth "Polenta" *with* Hearty Olive *and* Tuna Sauce

122   Crunchy Rice Cake–Crusted Halibut *with* Tofu-Dill Sauce

124   Peruvian Quinoa Shrimp Chicharrones *with* Green Aji Sauce

126   Thai Coconut Fried Rice *with* Basil *and* Tofu *or* Shrimp

128   Red Rice California Rolls *with* King Crab

130   Salmon *and* Buckwheat Coulibiac

132   Steamed Salmon *and* Black Rice Dumplings *or* Gyoza

134   Mushroom-Dusted Chicken-Rice Timbales *with* Pinot Sauce

136   Rolled Chicken Breasts Stuffed *with* Prosciutto *and* Barley

138   Saffron Quinoa *con* Pollo

139   Polpette *with* Bulgur, Parmesan, *and* Sage

140   Chicago Deep-Dish Spinach Portobello Sausage Pizza

142   French Lamb *and* Rye Berry Braise

LEFTOVER GRAIN SCRAMBLE WITH CHEESE

LEFTOVER COOKED GRAINS CAN BE BREAKFAST, LUNCH, OR DINNER with this easy scramble. If you are so inclined, mashed tofu can stand in for the moistening and binding action of the eggs, and a sprinkling of sesame seeds can take the place of the cheese. I really like this with brown rice and broccoli, but any grain will do. Once you've made it a time or two, you'll be improvising with whatever moves you.

2 cups **chopped vegetables,** such as broccoli, cauliflower, shredded carrots, *or* zucchini *(leftover cooked vegetables will do, too)*	½ teaspoon **dried herb,** such as marjoram, basil, *or* thyme
1 cup **leftover cooked grain**	**Freshly cracked black pepper**
1 tablespoon **water**	2 **scallions,** sliced
1 large **egg,** *or* 2 egg whites	2 ounces **cheese,** shredded
Pinch of **salt,** *or* 1 teaspoon tamari *(optional)*	

Heat a large nonstick or cast-iron skillet over high heat. Spray with vegetable oil and add the vegetables. Stir-fry until softened. Add the grain and water to the pan, and stir until the water is absorbed and the grain is heated through.

In a small bowl, whisk together the egg, salt, herb, pepper to taste, and scallions. Add to the pan. Stir and scrape the bottom of the pan as the mixture cooks. When the eggs are cooked and the mixture looks dry, add the cheese, and take the pan off the heat to let it melt. Serve hot.

OKAY, ITALIANS DON'T USE SOBA IN THEIR PIZZOCCHERI—they make a buckwheat pasta and roll it out by hand. But I figured you might actually try it if it were a little easier, and enjoy the classic flavors of earthy buckwheat, sage, and cabbage, bubbling with aged cheeses. A whole wheat spaghetti could also be used, but only if you simply can't find the soba.

PIZZOCCHERI *(ITALIAN BUCKWHEAT NOODLE CASSEROLE)*

1	tablespoon **butter**
2	tablespoons **extra-virgin olive oil**
14	ounces **savoy cabbage**, thinly sliced (*6 cups*)
4	ounces thin **French beans** *or* green beans, trimmed *and* cut into 1-inch slices
4	cloves **garlic**, minced
2	tablespoons **chopped fresh sage**
1	8-ounce package **soba noodles**
½	teaspoon **salt**, *or* to taste
	Freshly cracked black pepper
6	ounces **aged fontina cheese**, shredded

Preheat the oven to 400°F. Bring a large pot of water to a boil. Melt the butter with the olive oil in a large sauté pan and cook the cabbage and French beans over medium heat. (*French beans will cook more quickly than green beans.*) When tender and golden, about 5 minutes, add the garlic and sage, and cook for a few more minutes. Take the pan off the heat. Cook the soba in the boiling water according to the package directions, drain, then mix with the cabbage in the pan, adding the salt and pepper to taste.

Lightly oil a shallow 1½-quart baking dish, and put half of the noodle mixture in the bottom. Top with half of the cheese, then the remaining noodles, and finally the remaining cheese. Bake for 10 to 15 minutes, until melted and golden. You can also make this a day ahead, refrigerate, and bake for 25 to 30 minutes.

THESE FLAVOR-PACKED WRAPS ARE FILLED WITH SWEET ROASTED VEGETABLES and tangy pepita quinoa. Quinoa is already a complete protein, and adding beans makes this a high-protein and vegan meal. If you want to add some shredded cheese, they are delicious that way, too.

WHOLE-GRAIN WRAPS WITH QUINOA, BEANS, AND ROASTED VEGGIES

8	ounces **garnet yam** *or* other sweet potato
1	small **zucchini**, about 8 ounces
½	**red bell pepper**, about 4 ounces
1	small **red jalapeño**, seeded *and* julienned
1	tablespoon **olive oil**

Preheat the oven to 400°F. Cut the sweet potato, zucchini, and bell pepper in ¼-inch-wide strips, then cut them into 2-inch lengths. Toss with the jalapeño, olive oil, ground chipotle, and salt in a 3-inch-deep roasting pan, and roast for 20 minutes. Stir the vegetables, then roast for 20 minutes more, until the zucchini is limp and browned and the sweet potatoes are tender.

½	teaspoon **ground chipotle pepper**
1	teaspoon **salt**
1	cup **cooked black beans**, rinsed *and* drained
1	cup **shredded queso añejo** *or* other cheese *(optional)*

1½ cups	**Mexican Quinoa** *with* **Pepitas** *and* **Cilantro** *(page 63; half the batch, without the added vegetables)*
4	10-inch **whole wheat tortillas**
	Salsa, for serving

Let the vegetables cool, place in a large bowl, and mix in the beans. If using cheese, add to the vegetable mixture. Divide the Mexican Quinoa among the tortillas, and then top with the vegetables, placing the fillings in a rectangular shape in the middle of each round. Fold the sides in and then roll the wraps. If making ahead, wrap each in foil, so that they can be reheated in the oven.

Serve with salsa.

THE TENDER SHORT-GRAIN BROWN RICE IN THESE ROLLS holds the lemony filling together, as you plunge each roll in the garlicky sauce. Black or red rices would work well here, and buckwheat or millet would create a completely different taste. This makes about 4 cups of filling, which is delicious as a salad if the rolling seems like too many steps.

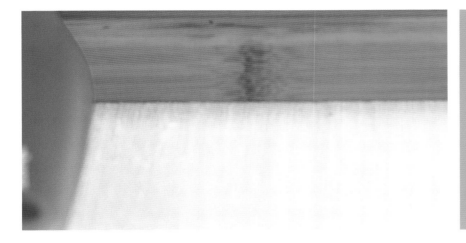

½	cup **lentils**
3	cups **water**, divided
½	cup **short-grain brown rice**, washed *and* rinsed
½	large **onion**, chopped *(about 1 cup)*
4	cloves **garlic**, chopped
2	tablespoons **olive oil**
½	bunch **parsley**, minced

MIDDLE EASTERN LENTIL RICE ROLLS
WITH **TARATOOR SAUCE**

1   teaspoon **freshly cracked black pepper**

Pinch of **cayenne**

1   teaspoon **dried oregano**

2   tablespoons **lemon juice**

2   teaspoons **salt**, divided

1   tablespoon **mild vinegar**

2   bunches **large-leaved collard greens**, about 24 leaves

SAUCE

½   cup **tahini**

2   cloves **garlic**, minced

½   cup **lemon juice**

¼   cup **water**

½   teaspoon **salt**

Sort, wash, and cook the lentils in 2 cups of the water. When tender, but not totally falling apart, pull off the heat and drain, rinsing very gently. In a small saucepan, bring the washed rice and remaining 1 cup water to a boil, then reduce the heat to a low simmer, cover, and cook for 40 minutes. In a medium sauté pan, sauté the onion and garlic in olive oil over medium heat until clear and soft; then add the parsley, pepper, cayenne, and oregano and remove from the heat. In a large bowl, mix the sauté with the lentils, rice, lemon juice, and 1 teaspoon of the salt.

Bring a large pot of water to a boil, and add the vinegar and the remaining teaspoon of salt. Cut the collards in half along the stem, removing the stem carefully. Drop the leaves in the boiling water and stir for 2 to 3 minutes, until softened and bright green. Drain and rinse in cold water immediately. Shake each leaf off and lay on a kitchen towel to blot dry.

Depending on the size of your collards, you can scoop a few tablespoons of filling on each leaf, then fold in the sides and roll up. Place on a platter, seam-side down. Serve at room temperature.

Use a food processor to make the sauce. Put the tahini, garlic, and lemon juice in the work bowl and process until smooth. Add the water and salt and process to make a pourable sauce. Serve with the rolls.

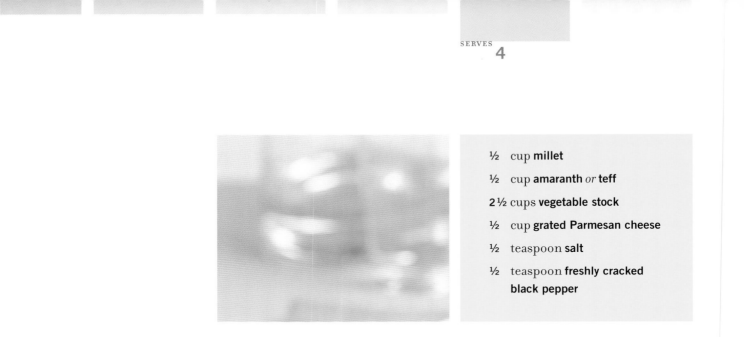

½ cup **millet**

½ cup **amaranth** *or* **teff**

2 ½ cups **vegetable stock**

½ cup **grated Parmesan cheese**

½ teaspoon **salt**

½ teaspoon **freshly cracked black pepper**

THIS FLAVORFUL SAUCE GOES TOGETHER FAST AND IS ALSO A GREAT TOPPER for whole wheat penne or brown rice, one you can pull together from your pantry in a pinch. Vegetarians can easily leave out the fish and still have tons of flavor. After trying this polenta, I can take or leave the plain corn kind; the flavor of these grains is so much better—in fact, millet was the original polenta, before Columbus. Teff, if you can get it, makes a chocolate brown polenta with a unique flavor.

AMARANTH "POLENTA" WITH **HEARTY OLIVE** AND **TUNA SAUCE**

4	tablespoons **extra-virgin olive oil**, divided		Grated **zest** *and* **juice** of **1** large **lemon**
4	medium **shallots**, chopped *(about 1 cup)*	1	cup **canned diced tomato**, drained
1	small **carrot**, finely chopped	1	6-ounce can **tuna in olive oil**, drained
1	teaspoon **anchovy paste**	1	cup **julienned fresh basil**
2	tablespoons **olivada black olive paste**		

Use olive oil to lightly coat a 9-inch square baking pan. Wash the millet, then combine the millet and amaranth or teff with the stock in a small saucepan with a tight-fitting lid. Bring to a boil, then reduce the heat to a simmer and cook, covered, for 30 minutes. Lift the lid and stir it a few times during cooking. After 30 minutes, it should be a thick, porridgey consistency. Keep cooking and stirring until it begins to form a more solid mass, about 5 minutes. Stir in the Parmesan, salt, and pepper. Scrape into the baking pan and smooth the top. Chill in the refrigerator for at least 3 hours.

Unmold the polenta onto a cutting board and slice into triangles or bars. Reserve.

In a large saute pan, heat 2 tablespoons of the olive oil and sauté the shallots and carrot over medium heat. When they are tender, add the anchovy paste, olivada paste, lemon zest, and canned tomatoes. Bring to a boil and cook for a few minutes, until thick. Add the tuna, stir it in, and add lemon juice to taste. Keep warm.

Preheat the oven to 450°F. When hot, place a heavy baking pan in the oven to heat for 5 minutes. Take it out, drizzle 1 tablespoon of the olive oil on the pan, and put the polenta slices in the oil. Drizzle the remaining tablespoon of oil over the top of the polenta, and place in the oven. Bake for 5 minutes, then turn the slices over with a spatula. Bake for 5 minutes more, until the edges of the slices are crispy.

Serve the polenta on plates, topped with the tuna sauce and basil.

CRUNCHY RICE CAKE–CRUSTED HALIBUT
WITH **TOFU-DILL SAUCE**

SAUCE

1   clove **garlic**

½   cup **fresh parsley leaves**, washed *and* dried

    Half of a 10-ounce box **firm-style silken tofu**

1½ tablespoons **fresh lemon juice**

1   tablespoon **chopped fresh dill**

½   teaspoon **salt**

¼   cup **extra-virgin olive oil**

A CRUNCHY COATING MAKES FISH EVER SO APPEALING, so why not use rice cakes? The whole-grain rice is an easy way to get crunch. If it appeals to you, try seaweed, sesame, or another flavor of rice cake; just don't go with chocolate! Vegetarians can substitute marinated tempeh for the fish.

2 **brown rice cakes**

1 large **egg**

1 tablespoon **Dijon mustard**

¼ cup **canola oil**

4 small **halibut fillets**,
  6 ounces each

First, make the sauce. In a food processor, mince the garlic and parsley. Add the tofu, and purée. Scrape down the sides and keep processing until it is completely smooth. Add the lemon juice, dill, and salt, scrape down, and process to mix. Pour the olive oil slowly through the tube with the motor running. Scrape the tofu sauce into a bowl and reserve, then wash the processor bowl, and dry it well.

Break the brown rice cakes into pieces and put into the food processor bowl. Pulse to break the pieces into rice-size bits. Transfer the rice cake bits to a pie pan or plate. In another pie pan, whisk the egg and Dijon mustard. Heat a large, nonstick skillet on high for a few seconds, then pour in the oil. Heat the oil until it shimmers. Coat the halibut fillets in the egg mixture, then in the rice cake bits, and put them in the hot pan. After the pan returns to a sizzle, reduce the heat to medium. Cook for about 5 minutes per side for thick fillets, less for thinner ones.

Serve hot, with the sauce in little bowls for dipping.

CHICHARRONES ARE A POPULAR FRIED SNACK IN PERU, and some chefs there are serving them with quinoa in the coating. This is a lighter version, using the technique of oven-frying to keep the coating from soaking up oil. The quinoa has a wonderful crunch, even without frying. I used red quinoa for a dramatic look, but regular quinoa will work just as well.

PERUVIAN QUINOA SHRIMP CHICHARRONES
WITH **GREEN AJI SAUCE**

SAUCE

1	large **jalapeño chile**, seeded
2	cloves **garlic**
1	bunch **cilantro**, cleaned *and* stemmed (*2 cups leaves*)
2	tablespoons **lime juice**
¼	teaspoon **salt**
¼	cup **extra-virgin olive oil**

½	cup **red quinoa**, rinsed
16	**jumbo shrimp** *or* prawns, tails on, deveined
½	teaspoon **dried oregano**
½	teaspoon **ground cumin**
¼	teaspoon **cayenne**
½	cup **unbleached white flour**
2	large **eggs**, lightly beaten

Make the sauce first. In a food processor or blender, finely mince the jalapeño, garlic, and cilantro. Add the lime juice and salt, and purée. Drizzle in the olive oil to make a smooth sauce. Reserve.

Bring a large pot of water to a boil. After rinsing the quinoa, add it to the boiling water and cook for 10 minutes, then drain. Spread the quinoa out on a baking sheet lined with paper towels to dry. It should be quite dry to the touch; pat it with towels if necessary.

Pat the shrimp dry, if damp, and put it in a medium bowl. Mix the oregano, cumin, and cayenne and sprinkle over the shrimp; toss to coat.

Preheat the oven to 425°F. Prepare 2 pie pans, one with the flour, one with the beaten eggs. Dip the shrimp in the flour, then the egg, then the quinoa. Place 2 heavy baking pans in the hot oven for 5 minutes. Take each out, spray liberally with oil, then quickly place the shrimp on the hot pans, keeping them from touching. Spray the coated shrimp with oil, and bake for 5 minutes. Flip the shrimp with tongs, then bake for 5 minutes more. Cut one through the thickest part to make sure they are cooked through. The baking time will vary with the size of the shrimp.

Serve the shrimp hot with the aji sauce.

COOKING YOUR WHOLE-GRAIN RICE IN COCONUT MILK makes it rich and flavorful. This meal-in-a-wok is a great way to showcase a fine rice, and it can be as spicy as you like. Just add more red pepper flakes, or if you have access to Thai shrimp paste with chiles, use that in their place.

THAI COCONUT FRIED RICE WITH BASIL AND TOFU OR SHRIMP

2	cups **coconut milk**
1	stalk **lemongrass**, bruised
½	cup **water**
½	teaspoon **salt**
1	cup **black, red,** *or* **brown rice**
1	pound **firm tofu** *or* shrimp
2	tablespoons **soy sauce** *or* fish sauce
3	tablespoons **lime juice**
1	tablespoon **brown sugar** *or* palm sugar
2	tablespoons **peanut oil** *or* canola oil
4	medium **shallots,** thinly sliced (*1 cup*)

½ teaspoon **red pepper flakes**
or Thai shrimp paste

1 tablespoon **chopped ginger**

3 cloves **garlic**, chopped

2 large **eggs**

4 ounces **snow peas**, trimmed
(*2 cups*)

3 large **scallions**, cut into
1-inch lengths

½ cup **fresh Thai basil**, washed
and dried

½ cup **roasted, unsalted peanuts**,
chopped

In a 4-quart saucepan with a tight-fitting lid, bring the coconut milk, lemongrass, water, and salt to a boil. Add the rice, return to a boil, then reduce the heat to a low simmer. Cover tightly, and cook for 30 minutes. When all the liquid is absorbed, take the pan off the heat and let stand, covered, for 10 minutes. Remove and discard the lemongrass.

Drain the tofu and wrap it in a kitchen towel, then put a cutting board on top to press out some of the moisture. *(If using shrimp, peel and devein.)* In a cup, mix the soy sauce, lime juice, and sugar; reserve.

Heat a large wok until hot, then add the oil. Add the shallots and red pepper flakes and stir-fry over high heat until the shallots are golden, about 2 minutes. Crumble the tofu into the hot oil and stir-fry, scraping often, until golden and crisp. *(If using shrimp, add the shrimp and stir-fry until cooked through.)* Add the ginger and garlic and stir for a few seconds. Quickly add the eggs, then add the rice and the soy sauce mixture. Let cook, undisturbed, for 1 minute to set the eggs, then start stirring and turning the mixture. Add the snow peas and scallions and keep stirring. Cook over high heat until the egg is cooked and no longer looks shiny or wet. Add the basil and toss quickly, then scrape out into a serving bowl and top with the peanuts. Serve hot.

RED RICE IS DELICIOUS AND COLORFUL IN THESE ROLLS. If you use a more delicate red, like Himalayan, use the lower amount of water and be very gentle with the rice. If you use a rice variety with a harder bran layer, like Wehani or Italian wild red rice, use more water and stir to break the bran a bit, so it will stick together in the roll.

RED RICE CALIFORNIA ROLLS WITH KING CRAB

Wash the rice and put it in a heavy 1-quart saucepan with a lid. If using Himalayan or a shorter-grain rice, add 1½ cups water, if using Wehani, add 2 cups water. Bring to a boil, reduce the heat to the lowest setting, and cover tightly. Cook for 30 to 40 minutes, until all the water is absorbed. Take the pan off the heat and let stand for 10 minutes, covered. Scrape onto a platter or wide bowl to cool, fold in the rice vinegar, and cover with a wet towel.

To take the meat out of the crab legs, use kitchen shears to cut up one side of the leg and down the opposite side, then pull apart the shell. Pull out the meat in long pieces, discarding any cartilage and shells. Put the crab on 2 layers of paper towel to drain.

Peel and seed the cucumber, and slice in long, thin strips and reserve. Slice the avocado in half and use a paring knife to cut the flesh, in the shell, into thin vertical slices. Use a spoon to scoop out the flesh. Put a bowl of cool water by your cutting board and put a splash of rice vinegar in the water, for moistening your fingers. Have a dry towel handy.

If using a rolling mat, wrap it in plastic wrap, so the rice will not stick to the bamboo.

Place a piece of nori on your dry cutting board or rolling mat. Scoop a cup of cooled rice onto the nori. Gently spread the rice on the nori, moistening your fingers in the bowl of water as needed to keep the rice from sticking to them. Try to make a very even layer, leaving the top inch of nori exposed to seal the roll. On the rice closest to you, place one-fourth of the crab meat, making an even strip across the bottom. Squirt a line of mayonnaise alongside the crab. Above that, place a few avocado slices, then two cucumber slices. Sprinkle 2 teaspoons of tobiko across the crab. Use your fingers to dab a little water across the exposed nori at the top. Using your fingers to hold down the fillings, use your thumbs to roll up the nori, making a neat cylinder. Let the finished roll rest, seam-side down, for a couple of minutes. Repeat with the remaining nori and fillings.

Use a sharp knife to slice each roll into 6 pieces, wiping the knife between cuts with a damp cloth. Serve the slices on their sides, with wasabi, pickled ginger, and soy sauce.

1 cup **short-grain red rice** *or* **short-grain brown rice**

1½ to **2 cups** of **water**, depending on the type of rice

1 tablespoon **rice vinegar**

1 pound **king crab legs**, thawed

½ medium **cucumber**

1 large **ripe avocado**

4 sheets **nori**

Mayonnaise in a squirt bottle

⅓ cup **tobiko** (*orange flying fish roe*)

Wasabi, for serving

Pickled ginger, for serving

Soy sauce, for serving

1 tablespoon **butter**

½ large **onion**, finely chopped
(*about 1 cup*)

1 small **carrot**, thinly sliced

½ cup **buckwheat groats**

¾ cup **chicken stock**
or vegetable stock

1 teaspoon **salt**

8 ounces **salmon**, boned
and skinned

EVERYBODY LOVES GOLDEN, CRISP PASTRY, and this one is loaded with goodies. Our Whole Foods Market sells a wonderful whole-wheat phyllo dough, which is actually much easier to work with than the regular kind. Use the type made with white flour if that's all you can get. You can also substitute other fish, like halibut, cod, or even scallops. Buckwheat is the best here, but brown rice or quinoa would be good, too.

SALMON AND BUCKWHEAT COULIBIAC

1 tablespoon **coarsely chopped fresh dill**

¼ teaspoon **salt**

Freshly cracked black pepper

Olive oil spray

10 sheets **whole wheat phyllo dough**, thawed overnight in the refrigerator

In a medium saucepan, melt the butter and sauté the onion and carrot over medium heat until softened. Rinse the buckwheat and drain well. When the onion is soft, add the buckwheat and continue to cook until the grains are hot to the touch and fragrant. Add the stock and salt and bring to a boil, then cover and reduce the heat to low. Cook, covered, for about 20 minutes, until all the water is absorbed. Take the pan off the heat and let steam, covered, for 5 minutes. Let cool completely.

Preheat the oven to 400°F. Cut the salmon into roughly 1-inch pieces, toss in a bowl with the dill, salt, and pepper to taste, and reserve. Use olive oil spray to spray a baking sheet. Unfold the phyllo, take out 10 sheets, and rewrap the remaining phyllo for another use. Place the 10 sheets on a counter and cover with plastic wrap. Lay a sheet of phyllo on the baking sheet, and spray well with olive oil. Cover with another sheet of phyllo and spray to coat. Repeat until all the sheets are stacked. In the center of the rectangle of phyllo, arrange the buckwheat mixture in a rectangle, leaving 4 or 5 inches of border uncovered on all sides. Place the salmon on top of the buckwheat. Fold in the short sides first, then fold over the long edges to cover the salmon. Spray the coulibiac well with olive oil, and cut 3 slashes across the top for vents.

Bake for 25 minutes, until the crust is golden brown all over. Cut into 4 slices and serve hot.

STEAMED SALMON AND **BLACK RICE DUMPLINGS** OR **GYOZA**

BLACK RICE INSIDE THESE DUMPLINGS makes them more substantial, as well as gorgeous to gaze upon when you take a bite. Steaming the dumplings is a lower-fat alternative, but frying and then steaming them as gyoza gives them a chewy bottom and infuses the tops with broth. Vegetarians can use tofu instead of salmon, and season to taste.

¼	cup **black rice**
½	cup **water**
1	teaspoon **soy sauce**
1	clove **garlic**, peeled
1	tablespoon **coarsely chopped ginger**
2	**scallions**, chopped
½	cup **canned water chestnuts**, drained

8	ounces **salmon**, skinned *and* boned
2	teaspoons **cornstarch**
1	teaspoon **salt**
2	teaspoons **sugar**
2	teaspoons **shaoxing rice wine** *or* sherry
2	teaspoons **dark sesame oil**

	Cornstarch for dusting *(if making gyoza)*
1	package **round gyoza wrappers**
	Oil for sautéing *(if making gyoza)*
¾	cup **chicken stock** *or* vegetable stock *(if making gyoza)*

Bring the rice and water to a boil in a small saucepan, and cook for 25 to 30 minutes on the lowest heat, covered. Let cool, covered, for 10 minutes, then uncover and stir in the soy sauce. In a food processor or by hand, mince the ginger and garlic, then add the scallions and water chestnuts and pulse to chop coarsely. Add the salmon and pulse to chop, not purée. Scrape the mixture out into a small bowl and stir in the cornstarch, salt, sugar, shaoxing, and sesame oil. Chill until ready to use.

To make steamed dumplings, cut a 2-inch square of parchment paper for each one; you will need about 28. *(If making gyoza, dust a baking pan with cornstarch.)* Have a cup of water and a small pastry brush at hand. Arrange several gyoza wrappers on a dry cutting board. On each round, put a packed teaspoon of the black rice, then top with a 2-teaspoon-size dollop of salmon filling. Use the brush to dampen half of the edge of the round of dough. Pull up the edges as if folding in half, and enclose the filling. Pinch the sides with the fingers of both hands, and press

SAUCE

¼ cup **soy sauce**

1 teaspoon **hot sesame oil**

1 tablespoon **rice wine vinegar**

the fingers toward each other to make pleats. Flatten the bottom of the dumpling so that it sits upright. Put each dumpling on a square of parchment and put them on a steamer tray or plate. *(If making gyoza, put them in the cornstarch-dusted baking pan.)* Cover tightly with plastic wrap and refrigerate for up to a day.

Boil an inch of water in the bottom of a large pan, then put the steamer tray with dumplings over the water and cover. Cook for 4 to 5 minutes, until a dumpling cut in half is cooked through.

To make gyoza, over medium-high heat, heat a generous coating of oil in a large skillet with a lid. When the oil is hot, quickly drop in the dumplings, one at a time, so the bottoms will fry. When they are all crispy and brown, add the chicken stock and cover the pan. Reduce the heat to medium, and cook for about 4 minutes. If the gyoza are stuck to the pan, add a little more stock or water to loosen them. Take the pan off the heat, set it on a cool surface, and carefully remove the gyoza with a spatula.

Stir together the sauce ingredients and serve in small bowls for dipping.

THIS RECIPE CAME ABOUT AS AN EXERCISE IN MAKING FOOD WINE-FRIENDLY. Earthy mushrooms, toasty nut oils, and nutty grains are all very compatible with the ever-popular Pinot Noir, and using the same wine in the sauce clinches it. Short-grain rices and blends, millet, and buckwheat also stick together well for a timbale presentation like this.

MUSHROOM-DUSTED CHICKEN-RICE TIMBALES WITH **PINOT SAUCE**

SAUCE

- 2 cups **water**
- 2 ounces **dried mushrooms,** any variety
- 2 cups **Pinot Noir**

TIMBALES

- 2 cups **chicken stock**
- 1 cup **short-grain brown rice**
- ½ cup chopped **carrot**
- ¾ teaspoon **salt**, divided
- ¼ ounce **dried porcini mushrooms**

  Freshly cracked black pepper
- 8 ounces **boneless, skinless chicken breast**, chopped to bite-size pieces

- 1 tablespoon **olive oil**
- 2 tablespoons **roasted pumpkin seed oil** *or* dark sesame oil
- 2 tablespoons **minced shallot**
- ½ teaspoon **sugar**
- 1 teaspoon **cornstarch** mixed with **2** teaspoons **water**, *or* more if needed
- ¼ cup **finely chopped fresh parsley**

Make the sauce. In a 1-quart saucepan, bring the water, mushrooms, and wine to a boil. Reduce to about 1 cup by boiling over medium heat for about 10 minutes. Strain the reduction through a coffee filter, squeezing out the mushrooms, and reserve the liquid. Discard the mushrooms.

Make the timbales. Oil four 1-cup ramekins for molding the timbales, or oil a metal 1-cup measure. In a heavy, 1-quart saucepan, bring the chicken stock to a simmer, and add the rice, carrot, and ¼ teaspoon of the salt. Return to a boil, then reduce the heat to low and simmer for 40 minutes. When all the liquid is absorbed, let the rice stand, covered, for 5 minutes.

Grind the porcini in a coffee or spice mill until they are a fine powder. Spread the mushroom powder, ¼ teaspoon salt, and cracked black pepper to taste on a plate, and roll the chicken pieces in it to coat. Heat a large sauté pan over high heat, then add the olive oil. Sear the chicken, turn the heat down to medium, and stir to cook completely. Take the chicken off the heat, remove to a plate, and divide the mixture into 4 piles.

To the same pan, add the mushroom-wine reduction from the first step, the pumpkin seed oil, shallot, and sugar, and bring to a boil. Boil for about 5 minutes, until reduced to ¾ cup. Add the remaining ¼ teaspoon salt. Whisk in the cornstarch mixture, a little at a time, until the desired drizzling consistency is reached. You may need to mix another teaspoon of cornstarch with water and add it, if your sauce did not reduce very much. Take the pan off the heat and keep warm.

In each ramekin, or in the measuring cup, pack a single layer of chicken, then mix any remaining chicken with the rice mixture. If using one measuring cup for all 4 timbales, reserve enough chicken for the remaining 3, then mix the rest into the rice.

Divide the rice mixture among the ramekins. Press it in firmly with the back of a spoon. Hold a serving plate over the top of a ramekin, then flip it to unmold the rice timbale onto the plate. Form all 4 timbales, then drizzle the sauce onto the plates. Garnish with parsley and serve. *(The timbales can be assembled in the ramekins, then covered and refrigerated. Reheat by baking for 25 to 30 minutes at 375°F.)*

6   ounces **sliced prosciutto,** divided

1   teaspoon **olive oil**

½   cup **chopped onion**

1   teaspoon **minced fresh rosemary**

¼   cup **pearled** *or* **hulled barley**

½   cup **chicken stock** for pearled barley, *or* 10 tablespoons for hulled barley

1   tablespoon **finely grated Parmesan cheese**

4   **boneless, skinless chicken breast halves**

½   cup **white wine**

1   teaspoon **cornstarch** mixed with 1 tablespoon **water**

INSTEAD OF GRAINS SERVED ON THE SIDE, here they fill a rolled chicken breast with texture and flavor. This is a good make-ahead entertaining dish, easily assembled and then baked when guests arrive. It would be delicious with any number of grains, from quick bulgur to brown rice.

ROLLED CHICKEN BREASTS STUFFED WITH PROSCIUTTO AND BARLEY

Preheat the oven to 400°F. Reserve 4 slices of the prosciutto for wrapping the chicken breasts. Chop the remaining prosciutto to make ¼ cup. In a 1-quart saucepan, heat the olive oil, and sauté the onion over medium heat. When the onion is golden, add the chopped prosciutto and rosemary, and cook until the prosciutto is lightly browned. Add the barley and stock, bring to a boil, and reduce the heat to a low simmer. Cover tightly and cook for 25 to 30 minutes for pearled barley, longer for hulled barley, until the barley is tender.

Let the barley cool, and stir in the Parmesan. On a cutting board, lay out the chicken breasts. Using a sharp chef's knife held parallel to the surface of the board, cut from the thinner side of a breast into the thick part, making a flap that can be opened like a book. Repeat with all the breasts, then cover with a sheet of wax paper and pound each cut to make a thin sheet of chicken.

Divide the barley among the pieces of chicken, then roll them up to enclose the grain. Wrap each in a slice of prosciutto. Put the rolled breasts, seam-side down, in a casserole with a lid, with enough room that they are not touching. Pour in the wine, and cover.

Bake for 15 minutes. Uncover and bake for 10 more minutes, until a thermometer inserted into the meat reads 160°F. Transfer the chicken to a plate, then carefully pour the liquid into a small saucepan. Cover the chicken and keep warm. In the saucepan, bring the liquid to a boil over high heat. Whisk the cornstarch slurry into the hot liquid and cook, whisking, until clear and thickened.

Serve the rolls sliced, with the pan sauce poured over them.

CHICKEN WITH RICE, Spanish style, is called *arroz con pollo*. Quinoa makes a delicious change, and the shorter cooking time means dinner is sooner. Brown rice or millet would also be nice here, with cooking times adjusted accordingly. Vegetarians can leave out the chicken and add more edamame.

SAFFRON QUINOA CON POLLO

½	lemon		1	teaspoon **freshly cracked black pepper**, divided		½	cup **frozen peas** or edamame, thawed
6	whole **artichokes**		1	large **onion**, diced (about 2 cups)		½	teaspoon **saffron threads**
2	tablespoons **extra-virgin olive oil**		2	cloves **garlic**, minced		1	cup **quinoa**, rinsed
1	pound **boneless, skinless chicken thighs**, cut into 2-inch chunks		3	tablespoons **tomato paste**		1¾	cups **chicken stock**
1	teaspoon **salt**, divided		1	medium **red bell pepper**, seeded and chopped			

Fill a large bowl halfway with cool water, and squeeze in a tablespoon or so of lemon juice. Pull off the leaves of each artichoke, and discard. Pare out the hairy choke, trim around the artichoke bottom, and peel the stem, leaving only edible flesh. Cut each in half vertically, submerge in the lemon water, and reserve.

Preheat the oven to 350°F. In a large, heavy brazier or Dutch oven, heat the olive oil over medium-high heat and drop in the chicken chunks, then season with a bit of the salt and pepper. Let cook, undisturbed, for 2 minutes before stirring, to get a good sear. Turn the chicken and cook until both sides are browned. Drain the artichoke bottoms, pat dry, and add to the pot. Add the onion, garlic, tomato paste, bell pepper, peas, saffron, remaining salt and pepper, and quinoa and stir to coat. Cook, stirring, for 2 minutes, to soften the vegetables. Add the stock and bring to a boil, covered.

Put the pot in the hot oven and bake for 45 minutes, then check to see if the quinoa is done. If the quinoa is tender but there is still liquid in the pot, uncover and bake for another 5 minutes.

½ cup **red wine**	12 ounces **ground turkey** *or* beef	Pinch of **grated nutmeg**
½ cup **beef stock** *or* chicken stock	4 ounces **uncooked Italian sausage**	½ teaspoon **salt**
½ cup **bulgur**	¼ cup **grated Parmesan cheese**	1 cup **seeded, diced Roma tomato**
1 clove **garlic**, minced	2 tablespoons **minced fresh sage**	4 large sprigs **sage**, for garnish
½ cup **chopped fresh flat-leaf parsley**	1 large **egg**	

THIS BULGUR-STUDDED MINI MEATLOAF is a great way to get meat lovers to eat their whole grains. If you'd like, use the mixture to make meatballs, or even a full-sized meatloaf.

POLPETTE WITH **BULGUR, PARMESAN,** AND **SAGE**

In a small saucepan, bring the wine and stock to a boil. Add the bulgur and return to a boil, then cover and simmer for 10 minutes. Take the pan off the heat and let stand, covered, for 10 minutes. Uncover and let cool. Preheat the oven to 375°F.

In a large bowl, mix the garlic, parsley, ground turkey, sausage, Parmesan, minced sage, egg, nutmeg and salt. Drain the bulgur in a fine strainer, pressing down lightly to extract the liquids. Add the bulgur to the meat mixture and mix.

Oil a sheet pan, and divide the mixture into 4 pieces. Shape each into an oval about 3 inches tall. Bake for 20 to 25 minutes, or until a meat thermometer registers 160°F. Serve hot, garnished with the chopped tomato and sage sprigs.

DOUGH

1	tablespoon **honey**
¾	cup **warm water**
2	teaspoons **quick-rise yeast**
2	tablespoons **extra-virgin olive oil**
2½	cups **kamut flour** *or* **whole wheat flour**
½	teaspoon **salt**

FILLING

2	teaspoons **extra-virgin olive oil**
½	large **onion**, chopped *(about 1 cup)*
8	ounces **Italian turkey sausage**, crumbled
2	cloves **garlic**, chopped

CHICAGO DEEP-DISH SPINACH PORTOBELLO SAUSAGE PIZZA

KAMUT FLOUR IS A WONDERFUL, GOLDEN FLOUR THAT HAS A BUTTERY TASTE, but whole wheat flour will work, too. This meal-in-a-pie takes a little time, but it is loaded with goodies. Vegetarians can just use 6 ounces of portobellos instead of adding sausage. I engineered it to fit in a standard cake pan, but you can easily double it to make two, or to fit into one large deep-dish pizza pan.

1   medium **portobello mushroom** *(or 3 for vegetarian version)*, cap only, chopped

10   ounces **spinach**, washed, stemmed, and coarsely chopped

¼   teaspoon **salt**

½   teaspoon **freshly cracked black pepper**

½   cup **chopped fresh basil**

4   ounces **Asiago cheese**, shredded

½   cup **grated Parmesan cheese**

½   cup **store-bought pizza sauce**

2   tablespoons **minced fresh parsley**

Make the dough. In a measuring cup, dissolve the honey in the warm water *(see the yeast package for the proper temperature)* and add the olive oil. In a stand mixer, mix the yeast, 2 cups of flour, and salt. With the dough hook, mix the dry mixture and add the liquid with the motor running. Mix until the dough is pulling away from the sides of the bowl; if sticky, add a little flour. Knead for 5 minutes. Let the dough rise in an oiled bowl covered with plastic wrap; 30 minutes to an hour should be enough.

Prepare the filling. In a large sauté pan, heat the olive oil. Sauté the onion over medium heat until golden, the longer the better. Add the sausage and cook until browned and cooked through. Add the garlic and cook for 1 minute. Remove the mixture to a medium bowl. In the same pan, over medium-high heat, sear the chopped portobello. Stir and cook until the mushroom pieces are dark and have shrunk by half. Add the spinach and continue to sauté until it is wilted and the whole mixture is dry—too much liquid makes a soggy pie. Use your spatula to press the mixture in the pan, and pour off the liquid. Remove from the heat, stir into the onion mixture, and add the salt, pepper, and basil.

Preheat the oven to 375°F. Oil a standard 9-inch cake pan and divide the dough by cutting off one third for the top crust. Roll out the larger piece to cover the bottom and 1 inch up the side of the pan. Mix the Asiago and Parmesan and sprinkle half over the bottom crust. Top with the filling. Roll out the top crust and place it over the spinach. Pinch the two crusts together against the rim of the pan.

Bake on the bottom rack for 15 minutes. Spread the pizza sauce over the top, and top with the remaining cheese and the parsley. Return it to the oven and bake for 20 minutes on the top rack. Let stand for 5 minutes before slicing.

FRENCH LAMB AND RYE BERRY BRAISE

WHOLE RYE WAS HARD FOR ME TO FIND, until a local farmer started selling it to co-ops and restaurants in town. It's got a nice, peppery flavor that complements the lamb. Any of the whole wheat berries or hulled barleys will substitute nicely. Vegetarians can use seitan for the lamb and a vegetable stock, and cook it just until the rye is tender.

¾	cup **rye berries**, washed	
3	tablespoons **extra-virgin olive oil**	
2	pounds **boneless lamb shoulder**, cut into 2-inch cubes	
	Salt	

1	teaspoon **freshly cracked black pepper**, plus more to taste
1	large **onion**, chopped (*2 cups*)
1	14-ounce can **diced tomato**, drained
1	stick **cinnamon**
1	**bay leaf**

2	cups **beef stock** *or* chicken stock
1	cup **red wine**
	Zest of 1 large **orange**, pared in long strips
1	cup **chopped fresh parsley**

Soak the rye berries overnight in cold water. Preheat the oven to 300°F. In a heavy, 4-quart braising pot with a lid, heat the olive oil over medium-high heat for a minute. Sear the lamb cubes in batches, salting and peppering to taste as you go. Remove with a slotted spatula to a bowl.

When all the lamb is browned, drain the oil from the seared lamb back into the pan. Add the onion and tomato and cook until the onion is soft and golden. Add the 1 tea-spoon cracked pepper, the cinnamon, bay leaf, stock, wine, orange zest strips, lamb cubes, and drained rye berries. Bring to a simmer, cover, then bake for 1½ hours. When the lamb chunks shred when pressed with a fork, they are done. Add the parsley. Remove the orange zest and bay leaf before serving. The rye will stay slightly crunchy. Serve immediately or all week long.

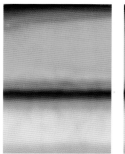
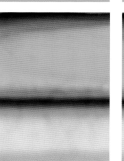
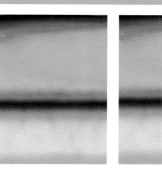

WHOLE DESSERTS

½	cup **unsalted butter**, softened
1	cup **brown sugar**
1	large **egg**
2	teaspoons **vanilla extract**
¼	teaspoon **almond extract**
1	cup plus 2 tablespoons **whole wheat pastry flour**
½	teaspoon **baking soda**
¼	teaspoon **salt**
½	cup **buckwheat groats**
6	ounces **semisweet chocolate**, chopped into ½-inch chunks

THE CLASSIC CHOCOLATE CHIP COOKIE IS A RIOT OF CRUNCH when whole buckwheat replaces nuts in the dough. Don't try any other raw grains for this—only buckwheat has a chewable texture.

CHOCOLATE CHUNK BUCKWHEAT COOKIES

Preheat the oven to 375°F. In a stand mixer or bowl, cream the butter and brown sugar until light and fluffy. Beat in the egg, vanilla, and almond extract until well mixed.

In a small bowl, mix the flour, baking soda, salt, and buckwheat, and add to the butter mixture, beating to incorporate. When the flour is mixed in, add the chocolate and stir until combined.

Drop 2-tablespoon-size balls of dough onto ungreased sheet pans, leaving 3 inches of space between the balls. The cookies will spread while baking. Bake for 6 minutes, reverse the position of the pans in the oven, then bake for 4 to 6 minutes more. A pale, soft center surrounded by golden brown cookie is the desired result.

Let the cookies cool on the pans for 5 minutes, then transfer to cooling racks with a spatula. Let cool completely before storing in an airtight container for up to a week.

THESE COOKIES ARE THIN AND CRISP WHEN FIRST BAKED, but will soften a bit in storage because of the maple syrup. The flavor of maple and orange zest are not only complementary to the oats, but they also have health benefits. Orange zest has been found to contain cancer-fighting chemicals, and if you can't get blood oranges, any organic orange will do.

MAPLE OAT CRISPS

½   cup **unsalted butter**, softened

1   tablespoon **grated blood orange zest**

½   cup **maple syrup**

1   large **egg**

½   teaspoon **vanilla extract**

6   tablespoons **whole wheat pastry flour**

¼   teaspoon **baking powder**

½   teaspoon **ground cinnamon**

     Pinch of **salt**

½   cup **old-fashioned rolled oats**

½   cup **finely chopped pecans**

In a stand mixer or large bowl, cream the butter and orange zest until fluffy. Beat in the maple syrup. Add the egg and vanilla and beat until well mixed.

In a medium bowl, combine the flour, baking powder, cinnamon, salt, oats, and pecans. Stir into the butter mixture to make a soft dough. Chill the dough mixture for at least 1 hour.

Preheat the oven to 375°F. Line 2 baking sheets with parchment paper. Use a tablespoon to scoop the dough, form it into balls, and place on the sheets at least 3 inches apart. A standard baking sheet should hold 5 cookies.

Bake for 6 to 7 minutes, reverse the position of the sheets, then bake for 6 to 7 minutes more, until the cookies have a dark golden edge that extends about ½ inch into the cookie. Cool for 10 minutes on the pans, then transfer to a cooling rack with a spatula to finish cooling completely.

THIS IS THE DESSERT I MAKE MOST OFTEN, because it is an easy way to use the best fruit of the moment. The perfection of ripe fruit with a buttery oat topping is both transcendent and homey. For a dressier occasion, bake this in ramekins and serve with whipped cream or ice cream. It also works well with other rolled grains, like quinoa or rye, if you can find them.

A **MACADAMIA FRUIT CRISP** FOR **ALL SEASONS**

1½ pounds **peaches, apricots,** *and* **plums** *(5 cups, pitted and chunked) or* 1 pound berries *and* chopped rhubarb *or* 1½ pounds apples *and* pears, peeled, cored, *and* sliced

Preheat the oven to 400°F. Pit and cut up the fruit, putting it in a 9-inch square baking pan as you go. If using berries, wash them well, pick over, and spread on towels to dry thoroughly, then transfer to the pan.

For the topping, in a small saucepan, melt the butter. Stir in the brown sugar, flour, oats, salt, cinnamon, and macadamias. Sprinkle the mixture over the fruit.

Bake for about 25 minutes, until the top is golden brown and the juices are bubbly.

TOPPING

½	cup **unsalted butter**
¾	cup **brown sugar**
½	cup **whole wheat pastry flour**
1	cup **old-fashioned rolled oats**
¼	teaspoon **salt**
1	teaspoon **ground cinnamon**
½	cup **coarsely chopped macadamia nuts**

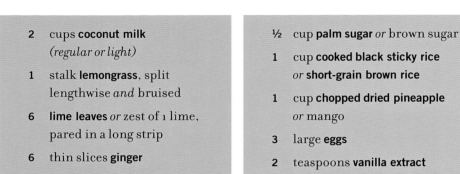

2	cups **coconut milk** *(regular or light)*	½	cup **palm sugar** *or* brown sugar
1	stalk **lemongrass**, split lengthwise *and* bruised	1	cup **cooked black sticky rice** *or* **short-grain brown rice**
6	**lime leaves** *or* zest of 1 lime, pared in a long strip	1	cup **chopped dried pineapple** *or* mango
6	thin slices **ginger**	3	large **eggs**
		2	teaspoons **vanilla extract**

EVER WONDER WHAT TO HAVE FOR DESSERT AFTER A THAI MEAL? This luscious tropical fruit pudding can be made with the sticky, stubby sweet black or brown rices to make it just as comforting and sweet as any dessert, or with any rice. If you have 1 cup of leftover cooked grain, just substitute that for the rice.

COCONUT-LEMONGRASS BLACK RICE PUDDING

Place four 8-ounce ramekins in a 3-inch-deep baking pan large enough to allow at least an inch of space on all sides. Bring a large kettle or pot of water to a boil, to make a *bain marie* for the ramekins. Preheat the oven to 375°F.

In a 1-quart pot, put the coconut milk, lemongrass, lime leaves, and ginger. Bring to a boil, cover, and reduce the heat to a low simmer. Cook for 20 minutes. Pour the hot coconut-milk mixture through a strainer placed over a large

bowl. Discard the lemongrass, leaves, and ginger. Mix the palm sugar into the hot coconut milk to dissolve it. Stir in the cooked rice and dried fruit. In a small bowl, whisk the eggs and vanilla. When the coconut milk has cooled to body temperature, whisk in the egg mixture.

Portion the mixture among the ramekins, making sure to distribute the solids and liquids evenly. Put them in the baking pan and pour the hot water in around them, so that it comes halfway up the sides. Carefully put the pan in the oven and bake for 45 minutes. Check for doneness by jiggling one ramekin; if the sides are puffed and the center barely moves, they are done. Take the ramekins out of the water to cool on a rack. Serve warm or chilled.

3 large **eggs**

½ cup **milk**

½ cup **maple syrup**

1 teaspoon **vanilla extract**

¼ teaspoon **salt**

2 ounces **unsweetened chocolate**, melted *and* cooled

1 cup **cooked buckwheat groats**

½ cup **semisweet chocolate chips**

THIS DEEP, RICH CHOCOLATE PUDDING IS LIKE A SEMISWEET CHOCOLATE BAR—not too sweet, but dark and satisfying. Get your antioxidants with unsweetened chocolate and grains, and have a good time doing it.

DOUBLE DARK CHOCOLATE BUCKWHEAT PUDDING

Preheat the oven to 350°F.

In a medium bowl, whisk the eggs, then whisk in the milk, maple syrup, vanilla, and salt. Quickly whisk in the melted chocolate. Pour into an 8-inch square baking dish or a 9-inch round dish. Sprinkle the buckwheat in the pan, pour the egg mixture over it, and then sprinkle with the chocolate chips.

Bake for 50 to 60 minutes, until a toothpick inserted in the center comes out clean. Serve warm or chilled.

SCOTCH OATS, SOMETIMES CALLED STEEL-CUT OATS, are chopped whole groats and have the benefits of whole oats with less cooking time. In this cake, they are infused with apple juice but still retain a chewy texture. Bulgur is also very good in this cake, and has just a slightly more assertive flavor.

SCOTCH OAT CAKE WITH **BROILED BROWN SUGAR TOPPING**

1	cup **apple juice**
½	cup **Scotch oats** *or* **steel-cut oats** *or* **bulgur**
1½	cups **whole wheat pastry flour**
1	teaspoon **baking soda**
1	cup **brown sugar** *or* raw sugar
½	teaspoon **salt**
½	cup **buttermilk**
¼	cup **canola oil**
1½	teaspoons **vanilla extract**

TOPPING

4	tablespoons **unsalted butter,** melted
½	teaspoon **vanilla extract**
½	cup **brown sugar**
	Pinch of **salt**
½	cup **chopped walnuts**

In a small saucepan, bring the apple juice to a boil, then add the oats or bulgur. Return to a boil, then cover and reduce the heat to a simmer. Cook for 10 minutes. Take the pan off the heat and let cool, uncovered. Preheat the oven to 350°F. Oil a 9-inch springform pan at least 3 inches deep or a 9-inch square baking dish.

In a large mixing bowl, whisk the flour, baking soda, brown sugar, and salt. In a medium bowl, stir the buttermilk, oil, vanilla, and oat mixture. Mix into the dry ingredients, stirring until well mixed. Scrape the mixture into the prepared pan. Bake for 30 to 35 minutes, until the top is golden and a toothpick inserted into the center comes out clean.

While the cake bakes, make the topping. In a small bowl, mix the melted butter, vanilla, brown sugar, salt, and walnuts. When the cake is done, place it on a cooling rack. Turn the oven to broil, and put a rack 4 to 5 inches from the heat. Drop spoonfuls of the brown sugar topping over the cake, spreading it gently and leaving ½ inch bare around the edges. Broil with the door open, watching closely, for less than a minute. When the topping is bubbling and melted, take it out to cool. Serve warm, after the topping has set.

IF YOU THOUGHT A WHOLE-GRAIN CAKE WOULD BE DRY, TRY THIS MOIST BEAUTY. It's like a cake with a pie on top. Nobody will even notice the whole flour, and you get the nutrients of pumpkin, apples, and whole grain.

APPLE STREUSEL–TOPPED PUMPKIN CAKE

3	tablespoons plus ½ cup **unsalted butter**, divided
4	large **Granny Smith apples**, peeled, cored, *and* thinly sliced
5	tablespoons **granulated white sugar**, divided
1	teaspoon **ground cinnamon**
1¼ cups **whole wheat pastry flour**	
1	cup **brown sugar**
½	teaspoon **salt**
2	teaspoons **pumpkin pie spice**
1	teaspoon **baking soda**
¾	cup **canned pumpkin**
⅓	cup **sour cream**
2	large **eggs**

Butter and flour a 9-inch-across, 3-inch-deep springform pan. In a large sauté pan, melt 3 tablespoons of the butter, then sauté the apples over medium-high heat until softened and browned in spots, about 5 minutes. Mix 3 tablespoons of the white sugar and the cinnamon in a cup and sprinkle over the apples, then toss and cook until the liquids are thick and bubbly.

Preheat the oven to 350°F.

Dice the remaining ½ cup of butter, and let it come to room temperature. In a stand mixer, combine the flour, brown sugar, and salt, and mix. Toss in the diced butter and mix until the butter is broken into small bits. Measure ⅔ cup of the mixture into a small bowl, and stir into that the remaining 2 tablespoons white sugar and pie spice to make the streusel.

To the mixer, add the baking soda and mix, then add the pumpkin, sour cream, and eggs, beating until smooth. Scrape the batter into the prepared pan.

Distribute the apple sauté over the batter, then sprinkle the streusel topping over that.

Bake for 40 to 50 minutes, until a skewer inserted into the center of the cake comes out clean. Cool on a rack.

THIS PIE CRUST CAN BE USED IN ALL YOUR FAVORITE PIE RECIPES; double it to make a two-crust pie. The whole wheat pastry flour is very absorbent, and if chilled for too long it will be very hard to roll. Just don't chill the dough for more than an hour, or overwork it, and you will have a tender, flaky crust.

WHOLE WHEAT PIE CRUST AND **FRESH BLUEBERRY PIE**

Make the crust. In a medium bowl, mix the flour and salt. Using the large holes of a box grater, grate the butter into the flour. Use your fingertips to work the butter into smaller pieces for about a minute. Mix the vinegar with the ice water and sprinkle over the flour mixture while tossing it with a fork. Try to press the mixture together, and if it is too dry, sprinkle in more water, a teaspoon at a time. When it just comes together, form it into a ball and cover tightly with plastic wrap. Chill for 20 minutes to 1 hour.

CRUST

- 1 cup **whole wheat pastry flour**
- ½ teaspoon **salt**
- 6 tablespoons **cold unsalted butter**
- ½ teaspoon **rice vinegar**
- 3 tablespoons **ice water**

FILLING

- 5 cups **fresh blueberries**
- ¾ cup **raspberry juice** *or* blueberry juice
- ¾ cup **sugar**
- 3 tablespoons **arrowroot**, *or* cornstarch, mixed with **2** tablespoons **water**
- ½ teaspoon **vanilla extract**
- 1 teaspoon **grated lemon zest**
- Pinch of **salt**

Preheat the oven to 425°F. On a floured counter, roll out the pastry to fit a 9-inch pie pan. Transfer the pastry to the pan. Flute the edges. Put foil over the crust and fill with dry beans or pie weights. Bake the shell for 20 minutes, then remove the foil and beans and return to the oven for 5 to 10 minutes. When it is golden and crisp, take it out to cool.

Make the filling. Wash the berries and drain. In a 4-quart saucepan, bring 1 cup of the berries, the raspberry juice, and sugar to a boil. Stir the arrowroot mixture into the hot berries, then quickly add the vanilla, lemon zest, and salt, stirring constantly. Bring to a boil, cook until very thick, and take off the heat. Quickly fold in the remaining berries and scrape into the baked and cooled shell. Chill until set.

PASTIERA DI GRANA *(WHEAT-BERRY RICOTTA CAKE)*

IN ITALY, THE LAND OF SLOW FOOD, a cake like this would have two pastry crusts, but I think the filling stands alone just fine. Nuggets of wheat and chocolate give the rustic ricotta cake a much more interesting texture. Farro or any of the larger, chewy grains would substitute well here.

½ cup **wheat berries**

3 cups **water**

1 strip **lemon peel**, 2 inches long, plus the grated **zest** of 1 large **lemon**

½ cup **honey**

2 large **eggs**, separated

2 pounds **ricotta cheese**

1 tablespoon **vanilla extract**

Pinch of **salt**

2 ounces **semisweet chocolate**, finely chopped

Soak the wheat berries overnight. Drain, and then cook them in the 3 cups water with the lemon peel until the wheat is tender to the bite. Let cool, removing and discarding the lemon peel.

Preheat the oven to 375°F. Butter a 9-inch springform pan. If your honey is very thick, heat it in a pan over low heat just until liquefied, then cool to body temperature before proceeding.

In a large bowl or a food processor, beat the egg yolks and honey just to combine. Add the ricotta and beat until well mixed. Add the cooked wheat, lemon zest, vanilla, salt, and chocolate and stir to mix. In another bowl, beat the egg whites until stiff. Fold the whites into the ricotta mixture, then scrape the batter into the prepared pan.

Bake for 45 to 55 minutes, until the edges are firm and golden and the center jiggles only slightly when the pan is gently shaken. Let cool completely, then chill.

Resources

BOB'S RED MILL

5209 Southeast International Way
Milwaukie, OR 97222
(800) 349-2173
bobsredmill.com
Hulled barley, amaranth, buckwheat, kamut, millet, quinoa, teff flour, red and white wheats.

EARTHY DELIGHTS

1161 East Clark Road, Suite 260
DeWitt, MI 48820
(800) 367-4709
earthy.com
Amaranth, black barley, couscous, wheat, millet, quinoa, spelt.

EDEN FOODS, INC.

701 Tecumseh Road
Clinton, MI 49236
(888) 441-3336
edenfoods.com
Whole-grain pastas.

NU WORLD

(630) 369-6819
nuworldamaranth.com
Amaranth.

PURITY FOODS

2871 West Jolly Road
Okemos, MI 48664
(517) 351-9231
purityfoods.com
Spelt products.

TIMELESS NATURAL FOOD

P.O. BOX 881
Conrad, MT 59425
(406) 271-5770
timelessfood.com
Purple Prairie barley.

WHEAT MONTANA

10778 Highway 287
Three Forks, MT 59752
(800) 535-2798
wheatmontana.com
Millet, kamut, oat groats, spelt, rye, wheats, brown rice.

AMAZON.COM

Amazon's gourmet food site has a huge assortment of hard-to-find grains, even Camargue rice and teff.

INCAORGANICS.COM

Black and regular amaranth.

Index

Table *of* Equivalents

The exact equivalents in the following tables have been rounded for convenience.

LIQUID / DRY MEASUREMENTS	
U.S.	**METRIC**
¼ teaspoon	1.25 milliliters
½ teaspoon	2.5 milliliters
1 teaspoon	5 milliliters
1 tablespoon *(3 tablespoons)*	15 milliliters
1 fluid ounce *(2 tablespoons)*	30 milliliters
¼ cup	60 milliliters
⅓ cup	80 milliliters
½ cup	120 milliliters
1 cup	240 milliliters
1 pint *(2 cups)*	480 milliliters
1 quart *(4 cups, 32 ounces)*	960 milliliters
1 gallon *(4 quarts)*	3.84 liters
1 ounce *(by weight)*	28 grams
1 pound	448 grams
2.2 pounds	1 kilogram

LENGTHS	
U.S.	**METRIC**
⅛ inch	3 milliliters
¼ inch	6 milliliters
½ inch	12 milliliters
1 inch	2.5 milliliters

OVEN TEMPERATURE		
FAHRENHEIT	**CELSIUS**	**GAS**
250	120	½
275	140	1
300	150	2
325	160	3
350	180	4
375	190	5
400	200	6
425	220	7
450	230	8
475	240	9
500	260	10